DISTANCING THE PAST

DISTANCING THE PAST

Racism as History in South African Schools

CHANA TEEGER

Columbia University Press
New York

Columbia University Press
Publishers Since 1893
New York   Chichester, West Sussex
cup.columbia.edu

Copyright © 2024 Chana Teeger
All rights reserved

Library of Congress Cataloging-in-Publication Data
Names: Teeger, Chana, author.
Title: Distancing the past : racism as history in South African schools / Chana Teeger.
Other titles: Racism as history in South African schools
Description: New York : Columbia University Press, [2024] | Includes bibliographical references and index.
Identifiers: LCCN 2024003300 (print) | LCCN 2024003301 (ebook) | ISBN 9780231213400 (hardback) | ISBN 9780231213417 (paperback) | ISBN 9780231559874 (ebook)
Subjects: LCSH: South Africa—Race relations—Study and teaching. | Post-apartheid era—South Africa. | South Africa—History—Study and teaching. | South Africa—Race relations. | South Africa—History—Historiography.
Classification: LCC DT1756 .T44 2024 (print) | LCC DT1756 (ebook) | DDC 305.8009680905—dc23/eng/20240125
LC record available at https://lccn.loc.gov/2024003300
LC ebook record available at https://lccn.loc.gov/2024003301

Cover design: Noah Arlow
Cover images: Shutterstock

For my parents, Alan and Rena
And for my partner, Dror, and our daughter, Ella

CONTENTS

1 Remaking Race and Nation Through History Education   1

2 Juxtapositions   22

3 Equivalences   44

4 Simulations   69

5 Consequences   107

Conclusion   126

Acknowledgments   137
Methodological Appendix   143
Notes   157
Bibliography   183
Index   197

DISTANCING THE PAST

Chapter One

REMAKING RACE AND NATION THROUGH HISTORY EDUCATION

SIYANDA WAS fifteen years old when we met.[1] In South African popular discourse, she is known as a "born free." Born into democracy, Siyanda is free of apartheid-era laws that disenfranchised blacks and discriminated against them in every aspect of life.[2] But to assume that she is free of racism and discrimination is to perpetuate a myth.

Daily, Siyanda traverses the racial geography engineered by the apartheid regime. She lives in Soweto—an urban area historically designated for black Africans. She commutes a total of five hours a day, weaving through the busy Johannesburg inner city and into its leafy green affluent northern suburbs, where she goes to school—and then back home again. Historically reserved for whites, her high school, Glenville, now looks like a microcosm of the Rainbow Nation—a term coined during the South African transition to democracy to promote aspirations of unity in diversity.[3]

But, on her long journey to school, in crowded minibus taxis and public buses, Siyanda is joined only by other black Africans. Many, like her, are students in formerly white schools. Others are domestic workers and day laborers. Describing the differences between Soweto and Glenville, Siyanda points to a disparity in resource allocation. In Soweto, she tells me, "there are no libraries at all," but in Glenville "it's a five-minute walk to the library."[4]

Siyanda's experiences of racial stratification and inequality do not end at the school gates. When I asked about discrimination at school, Siyanda related an incident in which a teacher refused to help her make up material and catch up on a test, even though she had a doctor's note explaining her absence. "Do you think you're special just because you're black?" Siyanda recalls the teacher asking her in front of all her classmates. "Do you think that BEE [Black Economic Empowerment, like affirmative action] applies to schoolwork as well? You're not special. You're like everyone here. You're not that much different." Reiterating her decision not to grant a make-up test, the teacher continued, "Just because you come all the way from Soweto doesn't mean that you have to be treated differently. It doesn't matter whether you're black or white, but you won't write your test."

In spite of this experience, Siyanda prefers not to dwell on the past or think too much in racial terms. This preference often puts her at odds with her father, whom she describes as stuck in an "apartheid kind of thing." When I spoke with Siyanda, she recalled a recent conversation they had. "You can't keep blaming them [whites] for what happened," she recollects telling him.

"You have to move on. If you want me to have a bright future, you have to let go. You have to teach me that thing is just over; that boundary is over, there's nothing left of it and [I] have to just work on like getting along with everybody, just not minding skin color, and just like move away from the fact that there was apartheid."

■ ■ ■

Why would a young black woman who experiences racial inequities every day of her life believe that the recent past of legalized racial discrimination should be forgotten, or at least ignored? This book points to high school history education as a key factor in this puzzle. In the pages that follow, I offer a granular on-the-ground account of how South Africa's first generation of "born frees" in racially desegregated schools were taught about apartheid. I spent eighteen months observing in history classrooms and talking with students and teachers in two former white schools, which I call Glenville and Roxbridge. As I analyzed these settings, interviews, and lessons, I learned that high school history lessons failed time and again to help students understand how the past informs, influences, and circumscribes the present. Instead, ironically, history lessons *distanced* the past from the present.

The lessons contradicted Siyanda and other black students' everyday experiences and masked the structural legacies of the apartheid past. To be sure, much has changed in South Africa. Yet even as a democracy, the country remains one of the most unequal in the world[5]—and that inequality is highly racialized.[6]

For example, less than 1 percent of South African households headed by whites live below the poverty line. In contrast, almost half of all households headed by black Africans (46.6 percent) live in poverty. On the other end of the distribution, while over 60 percent of whites are considered "skilled workers" (that is, managers, professionals, or technicians), this is true for less than 20 percent of black Africans.[7]

Advocates of race-conscious policies like Black Economic Empowerment (the affirmative action policy Siyanda's teacher mentioned) argue that unless we actively work to redress the past, these types of racial disparities will persist. The playing field, they explain, is not level, and no amount of ignoring the past will make it so. Siyanda, on the other hand, seems to argue the opposite when she says that "to have a bright future" she shouldn't focus too much on race or dwell on the past. The views Siyanda expresses are what the sociologist Eduardo Bonilla-Silva has called color-blind racial ideologies.[8]

Generally speaking, we can think of racial ideologies as the ideas and stories that sustain and reinforce racial inequality. Even when white supremacy is maintained through brute force, as it was during apartheid, there is always a racial ideology that underpins it. During (and before) apartheid, for example, an ideology about innate differences between the races was promulgated. According to this ideology, blacks and whites were genetically, culturally, and socially different from each other. For each group to actualize its potential, a policy of "separate development" was proposed.[9]

When Siyanda says that she needs to "move away from the fact that there was apartheid" and when her teacher tells her that "it doesn't matter if [she's] white or black," they are articulating a different kind of racial ideology. Writing about racial inequality following the U.S. civil rights movement, Bonilla-Silva identifies a range of supposedly race-neutral, "color-blind" beliefs that provide ideological support for an unequal status quo in the era of de jure equality.[10] Chief among them? The belief that, when it comes to racism, "the past is in the past." These color-blind ideologies suggest that today is all about equality of opportunity and that those who focus on race are creating and reinforcing racial divisions where none exist.

Ignoring both the realities of present-day racism and the continued effects of histories of racial oppression, these ideologies frame efforts to remediate past injustices as attempts to confer unfair special advantages. They describe race-conscious policies as forms of "reverse racism." By insisting that an unfair system is fair, proponents of color-blindness allow disparities to go unchecked. They also open space for the reinvigoration of racist explanations for racial inequalities (think, for example, of those who insist that economic disparities are just the natural result of differences in how hard different groups of people work).

How do people learn to be "color-blind"? Researchers have long assumed that young people are socialized into these views, but there is surprisingly little research documenting these processes.[11] Heeding Bonilla-Silva's call for further research on racial socialization,[12] my book draws upon a unique dataset that allows me to trace how, within one generation of democracy, South African students were socialized into believing that their country's racist authoritarian past has little relevance for understanding enduring racial inequality in the present. *Distancing the Past* offers a rare, detailed account of the consolidation of color-blind ideologies via racial socialization.

In addition to documenting *how* young South Africans were taught to distance the past, I address the question of *why* teachers taught about apartheid in this way. While teachers in my study were worried that learning about apartheid would make white students feel guilty, they were especially concerned about the possibility of black students becoming angry or making claims based on the past. They coped with these challenges by teaching about the past in ways that hindered students' abilities to link it to the present.

But these lessons were not just driven by teachers' own motivations. In many ways, they also mirrored ideologies institutionalized during South Africa's transition to democracy.

INSTITUTIONALIZING MEMORY DURING TIMES OF TRANSITION

In 1994, a year before Siyanda was born, South Africa went from global pariah to international role model. Apartheid had been dismantled through a negotiated settlement, and Nelson Mandela was leading the new Government of National Unity as the country's first democratically elected president. People spoke of rainbows and miracles as they described the transition to democracy and the formal end of decades of white minority rule on Africa's southernmost tip. In conflict resolution circles, people even began to refer to "the South African Option" as a model of transition. Essentially, they presented South

Africa as a model of reconciliation, an example of forging a new national identity based on unity, diversity, and *ubuntu*—a mutual recognition of shared humanity.[13] But how had the land of apartheid, the last outpost of white supremacy in Africa, so quickly transformed its reputation to one of tolerance and togetherness?

To understand this reconstituting of national identity, it's important to understand the political nature of the South African transition. This was a negotiated settlement. International sanctions and internal resistance had brought the country near a boiling point, but an unexpected announcement would tip it toward democracy. On February 11, 1990, at the opening of Parliament, President F. W. de Klerk announced that he was unbanning resistance organizations and releasing political prisoners. Nine days later, Nelson Mandela—South Africa's most famous political prisoner—walked free after twenty-seven years of incarceration.

Though the transition to democracy is often described as "peaceful," it was anything but. Four years of negotiations were marked by violence and assassinations by right-wing white extremists that threatened to derail the process.[14] At the same time, the country saw the eruption of so-called black-on-black interethnic violence.[15] We now know that this "black-on-black" violence was fueled by what became known as the Third Force operating within the apartheid government, which was deliberately aimed at destabilizing the negotiations process.[16]

Under these conditions, negotiators had to compromise. One of the major compromises was about how to deal with the past.[17] Members of the outgoing regime clearly did not want to be held accountable for their actions, but members of the incoming regime insisted on it. Ultimately, negotiators settled on amnesty for those who had committed gross human rights violations, but this amnesty was conditional on their providing a full and truthful account of their actions and showing that these actions had been politically motivated.

The decision to grant individual amnesty is one of the cornerstones of "the South African Option" in that it proposes a mode of dealing with the past that moves beyond retribution but does not sink into collective amnesia the way blanket amnesty might.[18] Commentators have praised this decision, arguing that it allowed South Africans to acknowledge the past without reigniting conflict.[19] Through the mechanism of the Truth and Reconciliation Commission (TRC), the brutality of the past could be examined in a way that fostered reconciliation and peace in the present.

Scholarship critical of the TRC argues that the imperatives around reconciliation structured a very particular engagement with "the truth" of South Africa's past. For example, instead of examining the everyday structural violence of segregation, economic exploitation, and unequal education, the TRC had a much narrower mandate. Its focus was on *individuals* who had committed gross violations of human rights. In an incisive critique, the academic and political commentator Mahmood Mamdani argues that, in focusing on individuals rather than on institutions or groups, the TRC "invited beneficiaries to join victims in public outrage against perpetrators."[20] In addition, the TRC had to decide what to do with members of resistance organizations who had engaged in violent resistance, ultimately determining that they, too, had to apply for amnesty.[21] A type of moral equivalence was thus constructed between apartheid's enforcers and its resisters.

These were not just legal decisions. They helped establish a foundation for national identity. All groups tell stories about who they are. When these groups comprise people who have never met face-to-face (and likely never will), these stories help create what the nationalism scholar Benedict Anderson has called "imagined communities."[22] As the TRC helped imagine the new South Africa, it constructed a historical narrative that framed apartheid as a time when individuals—across the political spectrum—did terrible things. This narrative allowed the majority of white South Africans to distance themselves from the brutality of the past and unite with black South Africans in expressing horror at the crimes that had been committed in their names—crimes from which they continued to benefit.

At the same time as it *individualized* accountability, the TRC *collectivized* suffering. In his detailed analysis of the TRC's public hearings, the anthropologist and transitional justice scholar Richard A. Wilson documents how commissioners worked to reinterpret the suffering of individual victims in collective terms so that it would be "shared by all, and merge into a wider narrative of national redemption."[23] A healing metaphor saturated the TRC, and posters with phrases like "healing our past" and "revealing is healing" spread this message across the country. By expanding the suffering outward from the individual to the community and the nation, the TRC suggested that all South Africans, black and white, suffered because of apartheid. It contrasted the racial animosity of the past with the racial unity and healing of the present. Focusing on both truth and reconciliation, the TRC dealt with the past—but it did so in ways that highlighted differences from, rather than continuities with, the present.[24]

Evidence from a large-scale survey conducted among a representative sample of South Africans at the time shows that the TRC process did indeed lead to feelings of reconciliation across racial groups.[25] But what about the next generation of South Africans, who did not live through apartheid and have no memory of the TRC? What do they know about the past, and how might history figure into their racial identities and attitudes? In recent years, critical discourses around the TRC and the Mandela presidency's reconciliation ideology have proliferated; and new political parties and social movements have pointed to the ideological work that reconciliation has done in preserving "economic apartheid" after the demise of "political apartheid."[26]

These types of challenges very rarely made their way into the post-apartheid history classrooms I observed. When they did, teachers were quick to shut them down. At both schools, I saw how history teachers toed the TRC line, deploying its narratives in ways that seemed designed to prevent the types of claims advanced by groups critical of the reconciliation process. For scholars of conflict resolution, these findings push us to think about the long-term and microlevel effects of narratives institutionalized during times of transition. For scholars of race and education, they expand our knowledge of schools as institutions that teach young people about race and inequality in an era of civil liberties.

LEARNING ABOUT RACE AND INEQUALITY IN SCHOOL

Schools stand alongside families as the most crucial sites of racial socialization. The sociologist Amanda E. Lewis puts it well: "race is not a fixed characteristic that [students] bring to schools with them and take away unaffected and intact. Something happens in schools . . . that forms and changes people in racial terms."[27] That "something" is not only students' growing awareness of their own racial identities in relation to others, but also the broader lessons they absorb about the racial order. Many of these lessons are implicit, part of what scholars call the hidden curriculum.[28]

Unlike the official curriculum (formal content covered in classes), the hidden curriculum includes the subtle lessons that students learn more informally. These lessons aren't explicitly taught and tested, but they structure students' understandings of race, identity, and inequality. Documenting the hidden curriculum means reading between the lines, looking at what is said as well as what is not said. It also means thinking about schools as holistic institutions—not just as places where students learn discrete skills like reading, writing, and arithmetic.

Focusing on the hidden curriculum, researchers have identified a variety of ways in which schools reproduce racial boundaries and hierarchies. Sometimes these processes are unintentional, occurring, as Lewis and Diamond put it, "despite the best intentions."[29] For example, studies have shown that in attempting not to appear racist, many white teachers become "colormute."[30] However, by refusing to talk about race, they do not make race or racism disappear. Instead, they create a context in which it is impossible to deal with the unique challenges that students of color may be confronting at school; and they teach young people that talking about race and inequality is impolite and risky.

Other researchers point to apparently race-neutral practices, like tracking, and how they implicitly teach students to link whiteness with achievement.[31] Messages about belonging and exclusion are further reinforced by school practices that overly discipline black youth[32] and privilege the cultural tastes, interactional styles, and emotional well-being of white children from middle-class families.[33] In a crucial comparative study of schooling in South Africa and the United States, the sociologist Prudence L. Carter explains that all schools have a resource (material) context and a sociocultural context.[34] School desegregation in both South Africa and the United States has opened resource-rich schools to black youth, while the sociocultural context has all too often remained untransformed, reminding us that desegregation is not the same as integration.[35]

To document the sociocultural dimension of schooling and the subtle messages it conveys about race and belonging, researchers focus on the lived experiences of young people within educational institutions. This means spending a lot of time in schools observing, interacting, and talking with students and teachers. Researchers often shadow individual students throughout their school day. Following students as they move from math class to English class, from the playground to the cafeteria, researchers document how lessons about race are woven into the fabric of the school day.

But certain classes teach lessons about race more explicitly than others. History classrooms are prime sites for this instruction because they present a place where individuals might learn not only about histories of racial conflict,[36] but also about the links between those histories and the current social order.[37] When history curricula mandate the teaching of racially oppressive pasts, classrooms become important spaces in which we can examine how people learn to talk about difficult issues they might otherwise prefer to ignore or silence.[38]

Most of what we know about history education comes from studies of textbooks that document what is included and left out of official representations of the past.[39] These representations are important because they can reinforce messages about belonging and exclusion. For example, James A. Banks, a scholar of multicultural education, has shown how, in U.S. history textbooks, black history is presented as "an appendage to the main story of the development of the nation."[40]

How do students understand these representations? Our knowledge about what happens once curricular guidelines and textbooks make their way into classrooms is much more limited. In her important research on young peoples' interpretations of U.S. history, the education researcher Terrie Epstein reveals that students' racial identities have a big impact on how they understand and evaluate history lessons received at school.[41] But we have yet to fully consider the role that history education might play in *constructing* these very identities.

This book looks at a very particular moment of racial salience as South Africa's first generation born into democracy confronted their country's very recent history of legalized racism in the formal education system. My findings point to the role of history education in muting racial boundaries in favor of temporal ones.[42] Instead of understanding themselves as members of racial groups with varying degrees of privilege and divergent relationships with a history of oppression, the students I spoke with articulated versions of color-blindness. They celebrated the irrelevance of race in present-day South Africa, even as many of them told me about the daily indignities of racism.

For many black students—like Siyanda—these views contradicted their quotidian experiences and delegitimized alternative interpretations about both the continued salience of race and the enduring legacies of the past. Whether black students truly believed these things is difficult to know. As researchers, we have access to what people say and do during the time we are interacting with them.[43] But we can't get into their heads. We don't know if they say and do different things at different times and with different people. This dynamic makes the social context in which our informants make their statements particularly important. Part of this social context of course is us—the researchers. Who are we? And how do our identities matter for what we see and hear? I am a white woman, roughly the same age as many of the teachers in the schools I visited. Although students seemed to trust me and, with the promise of confidentiality, told me about negative experiences with teachers in schools, I do not believe that my race or age became immaterial. Some of the black students I spoke with may have genuinely believed that the past is irrelevant, but it is very possible that they also believed that this is what they were supposed to say to white authority figures at school. Indeed, in both schools, the minority of black students who insisted on the relevance of the past for the present found their opinions invalidated by teachers, their attempted interventions into classroom discussions shut down.

So, what do these findings illuminate about race and inequality in school? First, they point to history classrooms as important spaces that transmit broad lessons about race and inequality. In teaching about the past in ways that hindered students' ability to discover and consider connections to the present, teachers reinforced notions of contemporary color-blindness, lending implicit ideological support for a racially unequal status quo. Second, my findings add to our knowledge of the unequal experiences that black and white students have in schools, as official subject matter reinforces and legitimizes the views and perspectives of dominant groups. Bringing the orientation of scholars interested in the "hidden curriculum" to bear on the "official curriculum," this study offers a detailed and nuanced analysis of the role of history education in reproducing racial hierarchies and inequalities within schools and beyond.

HISTORY EDUCATION AT GLENVILLE AND ROXBRIDGE

Glenville and Roxbridge High are top-performing government schools, boasting near 100 percent pass rates on standardized matriculation tests. Students earn commendations for their performance on such exams. Their sports teams excel. So many graduates go on to higher education that both are considered top feeder schools for one of the oldest and most prestigious universities in the country. These outcomes are not insignificantly conditioned on the legacies of privilege. The formerly white schools' acres of sports fields and swimming pools tell a story of uneven apartheid-era resource allocation and the way ill-gotten privilege remains privilege, even in the era of civil liberties. Under South African law, government schools are allowed to raise funds by charging fees; because they are in affluent suburbs, both schools, now formally desegregated, charge at the top of the range (though tuition is still substantially cheaper than at private schools).[44]

Glenville and Roxbridge also do well on what we might call transformation measures. Hallways lined with pictures of student leaders reveal a story of change—the school uniforms look the same, but as the portraits continue down the halls, the students' faces shift from all white to multiracial. These are the types of schools celebrated as microcosms of the hopes and aspirations of a transformed, multiracial South Africa.[45] In fact, their student populations are not only racially but also socioeconomically diverse. Recall that I noted the high tuition rates at Glenville and Roxbridge—that's not the whole story. Government schools in South Africa are allowed to charge fees, but they are *not* allowed to turn students away if they meet the admissions criteria but cannot pay. If a student's parent or guardian lives *or works* in the catchment area, the student is a candidate for admission. So, although both schools are in affluent suburbs, children from working-class families (often children of domestic workers) form part of the student body.

At Glenville, parts of Soweto fell into the catchment area, which meant that students like Siyanda could commute in too.

I chose these two schools because, in many ways, they represent "best-case scenarios" of history education in a multiracial, post-apartheid South Africa. To study the process of teaching and learning, I spent eighteen months between 2010 and 2011 talking to teachers and students and sitting in on classroom discussions. In designing my study, I aimed to tap the entire process of history education in schools.

To document the *production* of history education, I analyzed official national curricular guidelines as well as booklets that teachers distributed to students (neither school used a textbook; instead, they both created sets of notes that they handed out to students). I also interviewed all the Grade 9 history teachers across the two schools to understand the motivations behind their teaching practices.

To study the *transmission* of these narratives, I spent approximately four hundred hours observing in history classrooms. I usually sat at the back of the classroom and typed notes on my laptop. I tried to capture, verbatim, what teachers and students said alongside my own observations. Occasionally, students and teachers pulled me into classroom discussions; I detail some of these interactions in the pages that follow. For the most part, I observed, rather than engaged in, classroom interactions. While I do not believe that I became invisible or forgotten, I also do not think I presented a dramatic intrusion on the educational space. Both schools were used to classroom observation, often by preservice teachers and their supervisors, so my presence in the classroom was not wholly unusual (though its duration likely was).

Finally, to study the *reception* and *consequences* of these lessons, I interviewed 160 students. Of these, 82 were interviewed before exposure to the apartheid section in their history classes, and the rest were interviewed afterwards. I refer to the sample of students interviewed prior to learning the apartheid section as "pre" and to the sample interviewed after they had taken this module as "post." More information about these students, including how I selected them and what I asked them, can be found in the methodological appendix.[46]

Drawing on all these sources of data, *Distancing the Past* uniquely documents how official curricula are translated into notes, communicated in dynamic classroom interactions, and received and interpreted by students. Overall, this book tells a story about how institutionalized versions of the past are transmitted to individuals in face-to-face settings—and how these messages and collective memories matter for present social relations.[47]

OVERVIEW

The central argument of this book is that particular forms of engagement with history can construct the past as distant rather than making it alive and relevant for understanding the present. The next three chapters are structured around three main mechanisms of distancing that emerged in history classrooms: juxtapositions, equivalences, and simulations. Chapter 5 then identifies the consequences of this distancing for students' understandings of race and inequality in the present.

Specifically, chapter 2 begins with the official national curriculum and how it set the framework for what happened in schools. The curriculum embedded the apartheid section in a broader human rights module rather than situating it within a longer module on settler colonialism in South Africa. This decision resulted in a truncated historical narrative, limiting teachers' ability to offer a comprehensible causal narrative about apartheid. The juxtaposition of apartheid with the Holocaust, in particular, created a hierarchy in which the latter was ironically framed as more relevant to students than the former. In both schools, the result was that apartheid came to be coded as "boring" in opposition to the Holocaust, which was seen as "interesting." At the same time, findings reveal that boredom itself functioned as a placeholder for white students' refusal to engage with the legacies of South Africa's past.

In chapter 3, I largely focus on improvisations that teachers made in the context of dynamic classroom interactions. To minimize the potential for race-based conflict in the classroom and beyond, teachers constructed a type of equivalence, reminiscent of the TRC's engagement with the past, between apartheid's enforcers and resisters, its victims and beneficiaries. Over and over again, teachers in both schools emphasized that not *all* whites were perpetrators and not *all* blacks were victims during apartheid. Teachers employed this narrative to assuage white students' feelings of guilt and to limit black students' ability to make claims about the continued effects of apartheid on their lives. In trying to erase boundaries between "us" and "them," teachers taught students to draw a firm line between "then" and "now."

In chapter 4, I turn to a type of experiential learning found primarily at Glenville in which students were asked to simulate aspects of the past. Such practices have made headlines in other places too—such as in reports about a third-grade history teacher in Arizona in the United States who had her students berate an African American child during a lesson on school segregation.[48] At Glenville, for the duration of the apartheid section (approximately two and a half months), teachers required students to enter their classrooms and sit in rows segregated by race. Black students were required to show a "pass" (identity document) to enter the classroom. White students were not. In addition to trivializing the past, this simulation reinforced the idea that racism is a thing of the past and that students would not have access to the experience of being racially categorized and discriminated against, absent the simulation.

In chapter 5, I reflect on the consequences of this historical distancing for young people's understandings of contemporary racism. While many students believed that apartheid may have affected white and black South Africans who lived through it, they also suggested that apartheid's greatest enduring effect is that some people refuse to accept that it no longer has any real effect. In other words, students believed that it was time for South Africans to leave apartheid firmly in the past. People advocating for affirmative action policies (which many students labeled as "reverse apartheid") were, in their eyes, illegitimately holding on to the past. Because apartheid was taught as a history with no legacy, students were left with political orientations that opposed policies of racial redress.

In the concluding chapter of this book, I consider this study's implications for our understanding of race and reconciliation in a democratic South Africa. Other societies face similar challenges as they attempt to transcend their violent and oppressive pasts. For them, *Distancing the Past* offers important lessons about the complexities of moving past the past in ways that do not create blindness to its ongoing effects on the present.

Chapter Two

JUXTAPOSITIONS

"**HOW CAN** I help you?" asked Ms. Viljoen, a white woman in her early forties and the head of the history department at Roxbridge High, as I settled myself in her shared office. I was there trying to negotiate access to the school for the following academic year, having just completed my fieldwork at Glenville. Roxbridge seemed like a perfect place for the next phase of my study: similar to, yet different from, Glenville on a number of dimensions, including its student demographics. At that point, the main difference I had established was that Roxbridge enrolled many more white students: about 50 percent of the students at Roxbridge were white as opposed to 5 percent at Glenville. The comparisons that research access would allow were enticing: how did teachers and students in a different—yet still racially diverse—school grapple with the history of apartheid?

Ms. Viljoen listened patiently as I described my study. If granted access, my plan was to reproduce the methodology

I had used at Glenville High the previous year: I would interview a sample of Grade 9 students at the beginning of the school year. I would then observe in classrooms while students learned the apartheid section. And I would interview a second sample of students after they had completed the apartheid section.

My heart sank as Ms. Viljoen told me that my plan would not work. She quickly reassured me that she was interested in the project but that it would not work *logistically*. At Roxbridge, she continued, apartheid was taught in the first term, leaving no time to interview students before they studied the topic.

To be sure, my expectation that it would be simple to replicate my research design might have been guided by a naiveté—fieldwork can be messy and unpredictable—but it was not without reason. According to the South African Revised National Curriculum Statement (RNCS), Grade 9 history was structured under a human rights theme. In addition to apartheid, students covered topics such as the Holocaust, the struggle for civil rights in the United States, and the Rwandan genocide. At Glenville, the national curriculum was followed relatively closely, with apartheid taught, in chronological order, after the Holocaust. At Roxbridge, I was learning, this was not the case.

Perhaps sensing my surprise, Ms. Viljoen suggested that her school deviated from the more linear curricular guidelines because it aimed to make Grade 9 history as interesting as possible for students. Toward the end of Grade 9, she explained, students across the country elect their matriculation subjects, which they take until Grade 12. Having found that students especially enjoyed the Holocaust module, Roxbridge restructured the curriculum so that this section was taught during the crucial "subject choice" period.

It was so popular, Ms. Viljoen noted, that the school had scrapped all other modules in the curriculum, leaving only the Holocaust and apartheid. The Holocaust section—which took about a term to teach at Glenville—got most of the school year at Roxbridge, where it extended into a module on the factors that led to World War II. Although racist laws and policies had existed for centuries in South Africa, apartheid—as official state policy—was implemented in 1948, three years after the Nazi defeat. But because the topic was far less popular with Roxbridge's students, it was taught first, just to get it out of the way.

Later in the year, a new white educator at the school, Ms. Green, would express her confusion about the curriculum. "They've got it mixed up!" she told me emphatically. "We should be doing apartheid afterward." I asked her if she knew why the school taught apartheid first. Ms. Green responded: "I don't know. I don't understand it at all unless it's to do with—it could be because they know it's not as popular and that Grade 9s have got to choose [their matriculation] subjects . . . and to end on it [apartheid] might lower the numbers [of students selecting history as a matriculation subject]."

Ms. Viljoen's description of the curriculum presented a methodological challenge I would need to resolve.[1] I was not, however, particularly surprised to discover that a contrast was being made between the Holocaust and apartheid, with the former perceived as more interesting than the latter. I had found something similar at Glenville High. Educators at both schools seemed to have reached a consensus that students looked forward to and enjoyed the Holocaust section but found the apartheid section boring and did not want to learn about it. Many educators said that they believed students were surprised that, in reality, the apartheid section was not as boring as they had anticipated. All agreed, however, that—in the words of Ms. Prescott, a white educator at Glenville—"Hitler trumps them all."

Toward the end of my interviews with the post-sample of students from Glenville, I asked what they thought was the most interesting part of Grade 9 history. I expected this question to elicit a perfunctory response. The students had spent close to an hour discussing apartheid with me, and they knew that I was hoping to write a book on it. If ever there was a time to try to please the researcher by producing the perceived desirable response, it would have been then. And yet, over and over again, students earnestly answered that the most interesting section they covered in Grade 9 was what they repeatedly called "the Hitler section." Many told me that apartheid was "boring." How did this hierarchy of interest emerge? And why was apartheid juxtaposed with the Holocaust in the first place?

APARTHEID IN THE SOUTH AFRICAN SCHOOL CURRICULUM

Before history is delivered in schools and classrooms, it is constructed in official curricula. In South Africa, a national curriculum sets the guidelines for state schools across the country.

At the time I conducted my research, the curriculum was called the Revised National Curriculum Statement (RNCS). But this was not the first iteration of post-apartheid pedagogy. Indeed, one of policymakers' first undertakings after the transition to democracy was a restructuring of the curriculum.

Labor movements, then central in government through their alliance with the ruling African National Congress (ANC), played a crucial role in directing curricular reforms.[2] Rather than detailing and regulating the content that should be covered in classrooms, they advocated a focus on skills and specified "outcomes" that should be achieved at the end of the learning process. The resulting curriculum, implemented in 1998, was called outcomes-based education (OBE or Curriculum 2005). OBE integrated subjects into "learning areas" that were meant to equip students with the tools needed to participate in the global and regional economies that South Africa had reentered. History, seen as having little practical use, was virtually eliminated from the curriculum.[3] Moving away from the authoritarianism of apartheid pedagogy, teachers (now called educators) were given a lot of autonomy; and students (now called learners) were expected to be active participants in their own learning, rather than passive recipients of prescribed knowledge.

In 2000, the then minister of basic education, Professor Kader Asmal, commissioned an assessment of the curriculum. Stakeholders lobbied to reintroduce a clear focus on history,[4] with academics positioning themselves as key players in this process.[5] Following the formal assessment, the Ministry of Basic Education introduced the RNCS, which stated that it was "not a new curriculum but a streamlining and strengthening of Curriculum 2005 [which] affirms the commitment to outcomes-based education,"⁶ maintaining "a learner-centered and activity-based approach to education."⁷

However, the RNCS moved away from Curriculum 2005 in reinstating history as a key area of study, delivered through the social sciences learning area (which also includes geography). Social sciences were identified in the curriculum as central in the "development of informed, critical and responsible citizens who are able to play constructive roles in a culturally diverse and changing society."⁸ The RNCS Teacher's Guide singles out Grade 9 as a time to focus on history and human rights issues, though it retains educator autonomy when it comes to specifics.

Table 2.1 reproduces the content ("knowledge foci") provided in the RNCS for Grade 9 history. There isn't much there. Of

TABLE 2.1 Knowledge focus for Grade 9

The knowledge focus for achieving the Learning Outcomes in Grade 9 is reflected in:

- Human rights issues during and after World War II:
  - Nazi Germany: How did the Nazis construct an Aryan identity? How did the Nazis use this "identity" to define and exclude others? How and why did the Holocaust happen? What choices did people have in Nazi Germany?
- The end of World War II and the struggle for human rights:
  - United Nations Universal Declaration of Human Rights (including crimes against humanity);
  - United States civil rights movement;
  - human rights and anticolonial struggles in Africa.

(continued)

TABLE 2.1 *(continued)*

- Apartheid in South Africa:
  - impact of World War II;
  - what was apartheid?
  - how did it affect people's lives?
  - repression and resistance to apartheid in the 1950s (e.g., the Defiance Campaign, the Freedom Charter, and popular culture);
  - repression and the armed struggle in the 1960s;
  - divide and rule: the role of the homelands;
  - repression and the growth of mass democratic movements in the 1970s and 1980s: external and internal pressure;
  - building a new identity in South Africa in the 1990s: pre-1994 negotiations, the first democratic elections and South Africa's Constitution.
- The Nuclear Age and the Cold War:
  - Hiroshima and Nagasaki: the changing nature of war;
  - ideologies: capitalism and communism;
  - United States vs. the Soviet Union as superpowers: the arms race, conflict over territory, the space race;
  - the collapse of communism;
  - the collapse of apartheid.
- Issues of our time:
  - dealing with crimes against humanity: apartheid and the Truth and Reconciliation Commission compared with the Holocaust and the Nuremberg Trials;
  - xenophobia and genocide (e.g., Rwanda, the Balkans);
  - the effects of globalisation on Africa.
- A new vision for Africa: Africa's economic recovery.

Source: Revised National Curriculum Statement, Grades R–9, Social Sciences, 2011, pp. 61–62.

the RNCS's hundreds of pages, the section on social sciences is 110 pages. Just five pages delineate the social sciences content that should be covered for students from Grade R (reception, analogous to kindergarten in the United States) to Grade 9. The remaining 105 pages have to do with assessment standards, working schedules, and learning programs. In keeping with the principles of outcomes-based education, the topic areas are prescribed, but the details are left to schools and teachers.

The Grade 9 human rights module juxtaposes apartheid with World War II and the Holocaust, the U.S. civil rights movement, and the Nuclear Age and Cold War. Among a catch-all category titled "issues of our time," we find the South African TRC (which is to be compared and contrasted with the Nuremberg Trials that followed World War II), as well as xenophobia and genocide (giving the examples of the Balkans and Rwanda), and "the effects of globalization on Africa." The last-mentioned, like "Africa's economic recovery," the final topic of the curriculum, comes without any details or elaboration. Educators, it seems, are trusted to interpret these topics through a human rights lens for their Grade 9 learners.

The RNCS, under the reasoning that broader education should focus on universal themes, looked past chronology to group exemplary historical events under themes such as "nationalism," "leadership," "quest for freedom," and, in Grade 9, "human rights."[9] Curriculum developers could certainly have sited apartheid in a more traditional way—say, by spending a year's lessons on South African history and linking apartheid to what came before and after. Instead, policymakers' curricular design resonated with a desire to move past the apartheid regime's manipulation of history for nation-building purposes. Envisioning learners who were ready to enter a global economy, curriculum developers intentionally framed apartheid as a "case of" something (human rights abuses) and juxtaposed it to other such cases around the world and throughout history.[10]

In schools and classrooms, the resulting juxtaposition of thematic case studies translated into a hierarchy of student interest between apartheid and the Holocaust (as I saw when both learners and educators described a direct comparison between the two—and the perceived interest in each).[11] It also limited students' abilities to understand apartheid within a broader causal narrative that stretches backward to histories of colonialism and dispossession and forward to contemporary racial stratification.

APARTHEID VERSUS THE HOLOCAUST IN SCHOOLS

After making methodological adjustments, I was eventually able to gather the data at Roxbridge that I needed to compare findings with those from Glenville. In both schools, teachers presented a structural and psychosocial background against which to understand the Holocaust. They began by referencing the German defeat in World War I. Students did not need to have much historical background to understand that there had been a war, Germany was defeated, and the terms of that defeat—signed in a treaty at Versailles—crushed the German economy, angering and humiliating the German people. In this context, teachers explained, a man called Hitler found the right conditions to gain Germans' support.[12] Hitler promised to restore Germany to her former glory and identified a scapegoat for the nation's humiliation: Jews.

Teachers at Glenville added a psychological story about the development of Hitler's anti-Semitism. The handouts distributed to students explained:

> Hitler began to give the people of Germany what they wanted—someone to blame for their difficult living conditions. Hitler blamed the communists, the November Criminals (the people who signed the Treaty of Versailles) and most of all the Jewish people. Hitler's resentment of the Jewish people started when he was a young student trying to find a place at the Vienna Academy of Art. He was refused entry by the examination board [whose] principal was Jewish. In the years which followed his resentment of the Jewish people began to grow. Hitler promised that he would overthrow the Treaty, restore pride to the Germans and restore Germany to her former glory and more.

At Roxbridge, teachers did not give specific information about Hitler's anti-Semitism but focused on the conditions that eased his assumption of power. As noted previously, teachers at Roxbridge built up to the Holocaust section with a term-long module on the "Circumstances Leading up to World War II." One subsection toward its end was headed "Why did people support Hitler?" The handouts provided an answer:

> The Weimar Republic appeared to have no idea how to solve the problems of the Depression. The Nazis on the other

hand promised to solve the problems. Hitler promised most groups in Germany what they wanted. Hitler used the Jews and other sections of society as scapegoats, blaming all the problems on them.... People in Germany were tired of their poor quality of life. Hitler promised to make Germany proud again—it was exactly what people wanted to hear.

These sorts of "why" and "how" questions, no matter how cursory, were not used to situate the development of apartheid. Following the national curricular guidelines, teachers at both schools began the story of apartheid with "the impact of World War II." At Glenville, the notes opened with a question, "What was apartheid?" and provided the following answer:

> The 1948 elections occurred soon after the end of World War II. The general attitude after World War II was moving towards equality and ending racism. Many white people in South Africa feared that they were facing a future where the black majority rule was inevitable and that they would lose the lifestyle to which they had become accustomed. The National Party was aware of this fear and decided to use it in their 1948 election campaign.

Nowhere was it asked how whites acquired the privilege they feared would be lost. When several teachers at Glenville tried to introduce the difference between apartheid and what came before ("segregation"), their discussions were so unclear that I found myself writing in my fieldnotes: "kids are struggling with this (me too actually)."

JUXTAPOSITIONS

The notes at Roxbridge provided a more systematic explanation. "At the time of the outbreak of World War Two," they explained, "segregation was deeply entrenched in South Africa. There were many laws that prevented black South Africans from participating in the ownership of land and in government. Although the term 'Apartheid' had not yet been used politically, there was extreme segregation of the races." Further along, students read that "what South Africa under the Nationalist Party did was to make extreme racism and separation of the races legal in a time when most of the western world was moving in the opposite direction after the horrors of World War II and the Holocaust."

The schools' notes uniformly failed to explain how South Africa's racial relations of domination began; why they persisted when different sets of ideas were circulating throughout the globe; why apartheid leaders believed in what they did; or why white South Africans supported them. Instead—following the national curriculum—teachers in both schools began the apartheid section with the "effects of World War II on South Africa." Juxtaposing apartheid with the Holocaust, teachers narrated the former in terms of the latter. This meant that the story of apartheid seemed to start in the middle.

The sociologist Eviatar Zerubavel has argued that historical narratives—including where they begin and where they end—involve processes of social construction.[13] In this pair of top-performing South African schools, the RNCS had helped construct the history of the Holocaust as a self-contained story. This narrative centered on a charismatic leader who capitalized on social conditions by using the psychological processes of scapegoating and brainwashing, and it was neatly divorced from history except for the immediate terms of the previous war. This story is easily understood and, as presented, does not require deep knowledge about what came before.

In contrast, it was difficult to make sense of the apartheid story as presented in schools. Certainly, some histories may be more amenable to succinct causal narratives; as a rule, however, that is not how major historical events and eras unfold. And perhaps a story so close to home was inevitably harder to condense and clarify. But the teachers at Roxbridge and Glenville—again, as directed by the RNCS—presented a condensed account of apartheid beginning in 1948, and it left students confounded.

The victory of the National Party in 1948 indeed signaled a shift in South African race relations and subjugation—but in many ways, this was a shift in the *type* and *scope* of white supremacy. South African historiography has traditionally explained apartheid as the culmination of a particular form of racial capitalism that developed in southern Africa over centuries.[14] Teachers at Roxbridge and Glenville did not tell this story. Without looking at what came before, students were left without the tools to understand what was distinctive about apartheid, what factors contributed to the state-structured racism that it extended, or how its legacy affects contemporary South Africa.

So, what *did* teachers talk about in lessons about apartheid? Predominantly, they focused on lists of laws and events. Each school presented students with a list of apartheid laws, requiring students to learn by heart their precise names, dates of implementation, and provisions. The students were rigorously tested on this knowledge, along with lists of key events and resistance organizations.[15] The teachers often tried to build a causal narrative into the story by highlighting the intensification of resistance over time, but the primary organizing structure of the lessons was built around lists. Ms. Green, the Roxbridge teacher mentioned earlier, distinguished between the list approach and the narrative approach applied to these two human rights case studies:

> You know, [with the apartheid section,] they literally get a list of acts that were passed and then a list of how it affected the country, and then a list of how it went about to get changed. There's no—you can't explore anything in any kind of detail because they're so overloaded with these things [and they're] like, "*Ja* [yes] Ma'am, we know about that. We know about the segregation. We know about the Mixed Marriages Act. We know about the Group Areas Act. Like, give us another one."
>
> I really do think that they deal with Hitler in a much more intelligent way, and we should really start modeling the way in which you look at apartheid on the way in which you're looking at Hitler and Nazi Germany . . . [There] you're getting a theoretical—you're getting a timeline. So you're getting a chronological thing, but you're also getting a theoretical build-up. You can't understand Hitler if you don't understand what Germany was like at the end of the First World War.
>
> I think that's part of the problem, is that apartheid is treated as completely separate to anything else and it's treated as more important than anything else. But you can't understand it unless you're seeing it in the context of the country as a whole and our history before that section.

JUXTAPOSITIONS

To Ms. Green, narratives and stories stimulated student interest, while lists squelched it.

Other teachers also juxtaposed apartheid with the Holocaust when explaining student interest in history. Unlike Ms. Green, however, they did not connect a disjuncture in how the two histories were narrated to students' engagement. Instead, they suggested that students felt the apartheid section was repetitive of what they had learned previously. Students agreed with this interpretation.

HIERARCHIES OF INTEREST

"I think apartheid sometimes is hashed for them so much that they don't find it so interesting," the aforementioned Ms. Prescott told me at Glenville. That is, like the majority of the teachers I spoke with at both schools, she believed that the Holocaust was new to students and naturally interested them more than the apartheid section, which they'd encountered in school already by Grade 9. Ms. Viljoen (white, Roxbridge) concurred: "I think they start off, when they hear we're going to do apartheid, with an absolute mental block against it. They always will say things like 'But we've done it so many times' and 'Why do we have to do this again?'"

Students employed the same explanations in their interviews. I asked an African student, Lindiwe, who mentioned that she did not find the apartheid section interesting, why. She responded as follows: "I think because I knew about it. We've been taught [about it] since primary [school], so then you're always learning about it constantly. . . . Everyone knows apartheid, fight for freedom."

Lizzie (biracial) and Tammy (Coloured) concurred,[16] with Lizzy hinting at frustration: "We've learnt it like since grade four *ja*, we learn it over and over again. It's been drummed into us basically." Tammy seemed to suggest she was interested in the topic, but not in repeating lessons from primary school: "We wanted to learn new stuff about [apartheid], but they don't really give that. They just tell [us] stuff that we know. They just go more into it."

According to the RNCS, Grade 9 was the first time the country's students learned about apartheid, so I found it curious that the students complained of repetitive lessons. A closer look at the topics covered in earlier school years gave me a fuller picture. Not a topic in its own right until Grade 9, apartheid was touched upon under several history curriculum themes. For example, in Grade 3, under the theme of "Commemoration," students learn "stories about past events from the history of South Africa and the wider world." The RNCS suggests, as examples, Poppy Day, the Olympics, and two South African public holidays: Freedom Day (commemorating the first democratic elections in 1994) and June 16 (remembering the 1976 Soweto student uprisings).[17] Students in primary schools that chose the latter examples would have had some introduction—however rudimentary—to the story of apartheid.

In other grades, students learn about aspects of colonialism and dispossession in southern Africa that directly link to the apartheid story. Under the theme of "Industrialisation," for example, eighth-graders learn about "diamonds and gold, and the changing work and lives in South Africa on the mines, the land and in the cities (including the 1913 Land Act)."[18] The year before—in Grade 7—the "Moving Frontiers" theme included lessons about "contact, conflict, and dispossession in the Cape eastern or northern frontiers [of South Africa] . . . [and] in America in the nineteenth century."

Under the thematic focus of the RNCS, these aspects of South African history are rendered exemplars of broader topics, rather than inextricable pieces of a longer narrative of colonialism and dispossession that culminates in apartheid. Chopping up history in this way naturally gave students a sense of repetition, even though there was no narrative structure to tie the pieces together. This may be an unintended consequence of curricular reforms that focused on global themes and sought to include South African history among events from other parts of the world. But it also helped teachers avoid the sorts of *why* questions that might threaten to shift the conversation and lessons from the past and into the present.

AVOIDING "WHY" QUESTIONS

That a topic was silenced in the curriculum did not, of course, mean that students would not introduce it into classroom discussions on their own. Once, in Ms. Devin's (white) classroom at Roxbridge, the ninth-graders spontaneously got into a conversation about the origins of apartheid. There were only two pages left in their apartheid booklets, and students were busy

JUXTAPOSITIONS

learning about the 1980s, when I typed in my fieldnotes, "They are trying to understand where racism comes from."

A white student had raised her hand to ask, "Why were the blacks seen as inferior?" Another white peer had jumped in eagerly: "Yes, why was there apartheid?" Soon, typing furiously, my fingers could barely keep up with their questions and attempts to suggest answers. The classroom had become animated as students interjected, even forgetting to raise their hands as they usually did before speaking in class. "Maybe they were seen as a threat?" proposed an African student. "Maybe it was an excuse for white people when they came and took the land, so it was an excuse for them to feel they were right," added an Indian student. And a third white student offered: "When the Dutch came and became Afrikaners, maybe they felt superior cause they were colonialists."

Ms. Devin stepped in, asking, "Remember . . . *District 9?*" This was a science fiction movie in which an alien ship landed in Johannesburg, South Africa. "People were scared of the prawns," she explained. "I think it is fear of the unknown. The British came here; they hadn't seen blacks before, so they created these laws." The students challenged Ms. Devin. "But that is different," said a Coloured student, "'cause the blacks were here first and there, the prawns came." A white student agreed, adding, "I think that movie is more about the Zimbabweans coming to South Africa." But Ms. Devin stood her ground. "I think it's more about apartheid," she said. With that, she reasserted her authority and turned students' attention back to their handouts. It was time to read about international sanctions.

JUXTAPOSITIONS

This was one of the liveliest discussions I witnessed during my classroom observations, and it was all too brief. Students' interest was piqued by the causal questions of where racism and apartheid came from. In this discussion, students did not identify themselves with the historical actors whom they referenced. They used third-person pronouns, referring to "them" and not "us." Still, it's not difficult to imagine, if the conversation were allowed to play out, how students might move from past to present tense and from the third person to the first.

Ms. Devin's intervention pushed the discussion far from the realms of the present by creating an analogy with science fiction. But students brought the conversation back to reality. They reminded her that "blacks were here first" and referenced current xenophobia against Zimbabweans. These types of topics threaten to spill into the present, amplify divisions between students, and raise the stakes of the lesson. By minimizing *why* questions, teachers could limit uncomfortable conversations and the difficult feelings they might engender (including possibly for the white teacher herself).

In her interview with me, Zodwa, an African student at Roxbridge, also articulated a curiosity about the causes of apartheid and racial oppression in South Africa. Toward the end of my interviews with students in the post-sample, I asked whether there was ever a time in class that they wanted to ask a question but held back because they were worried about how others might react. Zodwa answered affirmatively. "There was a time," she told me, "where I've been like: Why did they do that? . . . Why did they hurt people like that? Why did they destroy so many families? . . . I've had those moments where I wanted to ask: Why did they do that?"

How, I asked, did she think other students would have reacted to these questions? Zodwa answered that she felt some students would want to know the answer, but others would prefer not to. "There are people in our class," she explained, "who feel that, let's just leave it in the past, let's just move forward and just forget about it." The "why" questions, in other words, pull the past out of the past, and they prevent forgetting.

In the case of apartheid, the curriculum itself was silent on these causal questions of motivation. But these were precisely the types of questions that captivated student interest in the Holocaust. Students were especially fascinated by Hitler and were very curious about what motivated him. For example, when I asked Nomvula (African) and Charlene (Coloured) from the post-sample at Glenville which section in Grade 9 history was most interesting to them, they both identified "Hitler":

> NOMVULA: I really enjoyed Hitler because, I don't know, it was just like—it's so interesting. You just look at him and say "What was he thinking doing all these things?" And you're just trying to figure out why he did them.

> CHARLENE: The most interesting [section] I think [was] the Hitler [one], the whole Holocaust and everything, because it's just so interesting to see how one person can do so much damage to a whole country, and how unfair certain people [can be] or how weird and silly some people's ideologies can be.

Doubtless, there are many, many problems with a historiography that overwhelmingly focuses on Hitler's psychology.[19] Still, these *why* questions—Why did Hitler believe what he did? Why did people support him?—propel the narrative and generate student interest, and they were notably muted in the apartheid section, with its focus on lists of laws and events. Students were not encouraged to broach "why" questions, and when they did so spontaneously, teachers tried to sidestep those discussions.

History is not just a set of facts. It is a narrative that connects those facts and attempts to unearth and learn from causal connections.[20] That's an interesting process, especially compared to how apartheid was taught under the RNCS, as if it sprang up from nowhere and, a half century later, was done forever. Still, when students referred to apartheid as a "boring" topic, they may also have used boredom as a placeholder—a more acceptable way to explain their unwillingness to engage with the ongoing effects of apartheid.[21] Recall how Zodwa explained her reticence to raise "why" questions in class; she was aware that other students "wanted to leave the past in the past." I followed up, asking her whether students said these kinds of things in class. "Well, they don't really say it," she explained, "but I can just see in their attitude, like they feel bored and all of that. I can sense that and stuff."[22]

■ ■ ■

Curricular reform in post-apartheid South Africa changed the way history was taught in classrooms across the country. The first new curriculum had all but excised history, but the Revised

JUXTAPOSITIONS

National Curriculum Statement, which was in place while I conducted my research, reintroduced history as a series of thematic modules. Shortly after I completed my fieldwork, another new curriculum was introduced: the Curriculum and Assessment Policy Statement (CAPS). CAPS condensed the content of Grade 9 history to include only apartheid and the Holocaust, the way history was already effectively taught at Roxbridge and at least slanted at Glenville.

When we assess educational curricula, we cannot only ask *what* is in the curriculum. It is just as important to know *where* and *how* topics are included. The juxtaposition of apartheid with other topics under the Grade 9 human rights focus limited teachers' ability to tell a causal story—to tell a *historical* story. Had apartheid been embedded within a module on settler colonialism and dispossession in southern Africa, teachers would have been able to explore the complex causes that led to the victory of the National Party in 1948 and how the party intensified and codified existing racist practices. Such discussions would have touched on issues of racism and economic exploitation that are as relevant for understanding the present as for understanding the past.

Instead, the apartheid story was truncated at both sides. This process of *historical truncation* severed apartheid's ties to the past and eschewed discussions of continuities. Apartheid was explained through lists of laws (that have now been repealed) and events (that are now long gone). Students were not encouraged to ask the sorts of *why* questions that would lead to an exploration of both the rise of apartheid and the continued salience of racism in South Africa, or that would connect the past to their own present lives.

Chapter Three

EQUIVALENCES

WHEN I began my fieldwork, I expected classroom discussions to be heated and animated. I thought that students might disagree with one another about the continued effects of apartheid on racial stratification in South Africa, that this disagreement might lead to conflict between students of different races, and that teachers must have to manage such friction frequently. On the contrary: instead of conflict in the classroom, I found a *fear* of conflict among teachers.

To manage the *potential* for conflict, teachers introduced narrative lines into their teaching that limited students' ability to make connections between past and present. Ms. Mokoena, an African educator at Glenville, described this approach quite explicitly in our interview. When she first began teaching, she had race-based conflict among students in her classroom. She modified her approach to prevent it from happening again. In the following quotations, italics are added for emphasis:

EQUIVALENCES

CHANA: Maybe you could just start by talking about what it's like to teach apartheid history.

MS. MOKOENA: It's a bit challenging. You've got to accommodate all the kids in the class. You've got to be sensitive to all the racial differences. You want to emphasize the wrongs that were done in the past, but you also want to, you know, not to make kids feel like it's their fault. So *you want to use the wrongs of the past to try and unite the kids.* . . .

CHANA: So what kind of things do you do?

MS. MOKOENA: Well, I normally highlight the fact that people that were struggling were not just the blacks; it was all the races. And I give examples of the people . . . from all walks of life, all races, and highlight how they suffered as well as a result of apartheid, particularly the whites. . . . What I noticed, particularly my first year of teaching apartheid, *I noticed that the black kids made the others feel responsible for what happened.* . . . I had a lot of fights. . . . A lot of kids started hating each other because, you know, the others are white and the others were black. *And they started saying, "My mother is a domestic worker because she was never allowed an opportunity to get good education."* . . .

CHANA: I didn't see any of that now when I was observing.

MS. MOKOENA: . . . Like I was saying, I think that because of the re-emphasis of the fact that, look, everybody did suffer one way or the other, they sort-of got to see that *it was everybody's struggle.* . . . They should now get to understand that *that's why we're called a Rainbow Nation. Not everybody agreed with apartheid, and not everybody suffered.*

EQUIVALENCES

> *Even all the blacks, not all blacks got to feel what the others felt.* So *ja* [yes], it's [pause] it's a difficult topic, *ja.* But I think if you get the kids to understand why we're teaching apartheid in the first place and *you show the involvement of all races in all the different sides*, then I think you have managed to teach it properly. So I think because of my inexperience then—that was my first year of teaching history—so I think I—*maybe I overemphasized the suffering of the blacks versus the whites.*

For Ms. Mokoena, the point of teaching apartheid history is to create unity, not conflict. Responding to the reality of conflict that emerged in her first history classroom, she adapted her teaching style by emphasizing that not all whites supported the system and not all blacks suffered under the system. This narrative diffuses the potential for conflict because it blurs the line between victims and perpetrators and dislodges the coding of "white = perpetrator" and "black = victim." If race does not denote culpability or victimhood, then students are less likely to make racialized claims about contemporary inequality that might spill into classroom tensions and hostilities.

Ms. Mokoena explicitly linked the reduction of conflict and the promotion of unity in her classroom to her teaching a narrative of equivalence. Other educators were not as explicit, but such narratives emerged saliently across schools and classrooms. Toward the end of my fieldwork (and as I detail later in this chapter), an educator would name the narrative of equivalence "both sides of the story."

There were two components to this narrative. First, educators highlighted that not all whites were perpetrators by focusing on white victims and resisters (beneficiaries were ignored). Second, they explained that not all blacks were victims by focusing on black perpetrators during apartheid. These narrative lines are powerful because they make it difficult for students to make race-based assumptions about historical actors—and, by implication, about contemporary ones. For teachers, they become tools to minimize conflict and to deal with difficult emotions in the classroom.

WHITE VICTIMS AND RESISTERS

In every classroom I observed, teachers emphasized that not all whites supported the apartheid system. While this is undoubtedly true, it is also true that between 1948 and 1994, the white electorate voted the National Party and its policy of apartheid into power on eleven separate occasions. Teachers did not mention this fact in class, nor did they fully explore why some people supported the system while others did not[1]. They noted that different people made different choices, but they did not discuss the motivations behind these choices. Along these lines, Ms. Prescott, a white Glenville educator, told me that she strives to get her students to understand "both sides of the coin." I asked her what she meant by that phrase, and she replied: "to obviously make them understand that it's not this black versus white situation, that there were whites who disagreed with apartheid and there were those that agreed, so they can get a whole idea of what it's all about."

Several of the teachers I observed at Roxbridge began the apartheid section with a discussion of stereotypes. Ms. Roux, herself white, concluded this discussion by reminding her students that not all whites were racist. She implored her students to "think about this the whole year," thus framing the forthcoming discussion of apartheid within the *both sides of the story* narrative: "Now, I want you to think about this the whole year. . . . Don't make up your mind about a group of people before you got to know the whole story. When we learn about apartheid, don't think all the whites were racists [and that] they all wanted everyone to suffer."

Ms. Roux implicitly framed the entire history of apartheid within an understanding of racism as individual-level prejudice rather than as a broader structural system of inequality.[2] Ms. Ndlovu, an African teacher at Glenville, also steered students away from contemplating apartheid as a system under which whites were beneficiaries by focusing on the exceptions: whites who opposed the system. Ms. Ndlovu taught four Grade 9 classes. In each, she recounted how she had once invited the parent of a white student to talk to her history class. Reflecting on this experience in our interview, Ms. Ndlovu noted:

> He wanted to show us that even whites were not happy about the system . . . and, you know, black students were so fascinated because they were asking him . . . "But you had benefits, why were you against this system because you were benefiting from the system?" But he was saying, "No, it's not about benefits. It is more about *ubuntu*, about being human."

EQUIVALENCES

Ubuntu is an African concept popularized by Archbishop Desmond Tutu during the days of the Truth and Reconciliation Commission (TRC) as a way to refer to a shared humanness that connects all South Africans.[3] In retelling the white parent's story, Ms. Ndlovu directed attention away from questions of privilege and failed to explore how one can oppose a system and at the same time benefit from it.

In their discussions of white opposition to apartheid, teachers did not distinguish between whites who joined resistance movements and those who disagreed with the system but did not do anything about it. By framing white resisters in terms of their thoughts and feelings (they "were not happy about the system," "they disagreed," "they were not racist"), educators created an equivalence between the small number of whites who put themselves on the line to fight against injustice and those who could claim ex post facto that they never liked the system. In these historical depictions, many white South Africans, like black South Africans, opposed apartheid.

Students were told not only that many whites resisted apartheid, but also that many suffered. In one classroom exchange at Glenville, I witnessed an African student ask his white teacher, Mr. Lane, if apartheid laws also affected whites. Resolutely, a fellow African student answered, "No." But Mr. Lane responded: "What happened if a white person fell in love with a black person?" The question was meant to provoke reflection on the ways apartheid also constrained whites' lives and loves. At Roxbridge, a white student asked Ms. Lesley, herself white, a similar question: "So, if you were white could you go where you wanted and do what you wanted?" Like Mr. Lane, Ms. Lesley responded: "Yes, but you couldn't mix with people of other races. If you marry them, then you'd be arrested."

In their interviews with me, students also expressed these ideas of white suffering. I asked Morris, a Coloured student in the post-sample at Glenville, if he could tell me who was oppressed or victimized during apartheid. He answered, "Well, I think everybody was. Everybody was oppressed and victimized, even the white people. In a way, the white people were also being oppressed because they weren't experiencing black culture, but now they're experiencing it, now they're enjoying it." Madison, a white student in the same subsample, similarly told me that "we all were [victimized and oppressed] actually." She continued: "not only the other races, but like the whites also didn't get to grow up with other races and stuff." Focusing on apartheid as a system of segregation—but ignoring issues of power and inequality—teachers and students constructed an equivalence between white and black suffering during apartheid.

As part of the process of dislodging the characterization of whites as perpetrators, teachers also explained that, during apartheid, many whites simply did not know what was going on. For example, Ms. Devin, a white teacher at Roxbridge, told her students that "a lot of times people didn't know about what was happening 'cause it was kept secret."[4] While this may have been true for some of the extreme forms of violence that came to light during the time of the TRC, whites certainly did know that only *they* could vote. They knew that blacks were only permitted certain types of jobs and had to live in specific areas. They knew that schools were segregated and that white schools were better. They knew that their black domestic workers lived in small rooms behind their homes and that they required permits to be there. They knew that blacks had to ride different buses, use different restrooms, and enter through different entrances. To say that "they did not know" not only lets these historical actors off the hook but also hinders an understanding of the pervasive and systemic nature of apartheid and its aftereffects.

Taking in this message, several black students told me in interviews that their parents were not *really* affected by apartheid. Nicole, a Coloured student in the post-sample at Glenville, for example, told me: "My mom went to a Coloured school. She lived in Westbury, so it was a Coloured township. So, she was never affected by it." Focusing on extreme acts of violence perpetrated by the apartheid regime led these students to suggest that their parents did not feel the effects of apartheid. The contradiction between whites being affected by laws because they could not love whom they wanted to love, and blacks only being considered to have been affected if they suffered extreme forms of violence, was missed by both teachers and students.

In general, students across both schools spoke about white resistance and suffering much more often—three times as often[5]—in the post-sample than in the pre-sample interviews,[6] suggesting that they had taken in their teachers' "both sides" rhetoric in the apartheid module (see figure 3.1). For instance, I asked Thandi, an African student in the post-sample at Glenville, whether learning about apartheid changed how she saw her white teachers. She answered in the affirmative, explaining that "some of them didn't like apartheid. They just wanted to mingle and talk to different races." I probed, wondering whether this was something she believed all along or if she

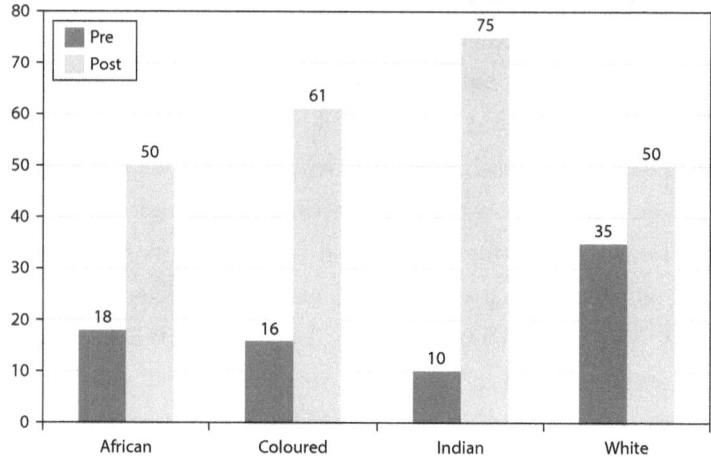

FIGURE 3.1 Percentage of students who noted that not all whites supported the system, by race and sample.

realized it while learning about apartheid in Grade 9 history. The latter, she said, "[the] apartheid [section] made me realize it." And when asked how, Thandi had no hesitation: she said she had learned in the past year "that it wasn't only us black people who were affected."

BLACK PERPETRATORS

The second part of *both sides of the story* involves complicating the characterization of blacks as victims. The clearest articulation of this idea came in discussions of the Pan Africanist Congress (PAC). The PAC, which broke away from the African National Congress (ANC) in the 1950s, led the movement from passive to violent resistance through the formation of its military wing, *Poqo*. The group's leadership argued that blacks should not rely on whites but rather take control of their own liberation. Teachers could certainly have used this idea as a springboard for interrogating the different anti-apartheid organizations' approaches to resistance and their visions of a liberated South Africa. Instead, they presented the PAC as a foil to South Africa's ruling party since 1994, the ANC.

Teachers used the fact that the ANC also formed a military wing, *Umkhonto we Sizwe* (MK), to establish the ANC's moral high ground by arguing that, unlike *Poqo*, MK attacked only nonhuman targets. This depiction of the ANC's armed resistance is not entirely accurate.[7] Nonetheless, using this contrast helped teachers construct a story about how some blacks engaged in activities that were morally equivalent to the most violent practices of the apartheid regime. They used the PAC's ideas about black consciousness to argue that, like some whites, some blacks were also "racist."[8]

This discourse presents apartheid as a conflict between two groups that, in the words of Ms. Viljoen (white, Roxbridge), "hated each other," rather than the story of one group that resisted oppression by another group. A discussion in Mr. Pretorius's (white, Glenville) class exemplified this framing and revealed for me a concept that students would later tie to current affirmative action policies: "reverse apartheid." Mr. Pretorius began his class by recapping the previous lesson, and in this instance, that meant starting by asking the students,

"Remember what the PAC stands for?" Instead of responding "Pan Africanist Congress," the students answered as a chorus: "reverse apartheid." Mr. Pretorius affirmed their answer: "Yes. And what race was only allowed to be in the PAC?" Students responded: "Blacks." Again, Mr. Pretorius told them they were correct, adding that the PAC "was trying to reinforce apartheid, just vice versa."

Ms. Viljoen made a similar point when she explained to her students that groups from across the political spectrum refused to participate in talks during the negotiation process that ushered in the end of apartheid. She drew a circle and a line on the chalkboard, telling the class that the political spectrum is more like the former than the latter. To her, groups on both ends of the "line" depiction of political belief were actually quite similar to each other, bending the line into a circle. On one end of the political spectrum, she said, were people who "want the old ways" and, on the other, were groups "like the PAC who had slogans . . . like one settler, one bullet—so to get rid of all the whites." Ms. Viljoen continued:

> And can you see how I drew my spectrum so the arrows come together at the end? They actually become very similar at the end, they believe in violence to get their way and they are very extreme. They say "only my way." *And they will hate each other.* But if you look at it on paper, they are getting quite close to each other in the way they do things, in their beliefs. *The one is saying the whites should have everything [and] the other [is] saying the blacks should have everything—same system, different colors.* (emphasis added)

EQUIVALENCES

At both Roxbridge and Glenville, I heard this story of PAC violence and ideology, and it was juxtaposed with a famous quote from Nelson Mandela's treason trial. Booklets[9] in both schools reproduce the following section from Mandela's speech: "During my lifetime, I have dedicated my life to this struggle of the African people. *I have fought against white domination and I have fought against black domination.* I have cherished the ideal of a democratic and free society in which all persons live together in harmony and with equal opportunities. It is an ideal which I hope to live for and to achieve. But, if needs be, it is an ideal for which I am prepared to die [emphasis added]."

What did Mandela mean, the teachers asked their classes, when he referred to "black domination"? In fieldnotes taken during Ms. Roux's class at Roxbridge, I captured a representative exchange:

MS. ROUX: What do you guys think?
WHITE MALE: He's neutral. He wasn't being racist. He had nothing against the white people.
MS. ROUX: Yes, because he fought against black people also. So for him, it wasn't a color thing; it was a thing of right and wrong. So the black people he fought against were the PAC and also the few black people who supported apartheid.

The narrative of moral equivalence reemerged in discussions of the TRC. In chapter 1, I discussed how the TRC required members of both the apartheid regime and resistance movements to apply for amnesty. In this way, the TRC itself can be

EQUIVALENCES

said to represent an earlier institutionalized version of *both sides of the story*. When teaching about the TRC, teachers advanced its narrative about moral equivalence, in which there were individuals both pro- and anti-apartheid who were in need of absolution.

In most classrooms, students simply accepted the narrative presented by teachers. However, in Ms. Prescott's (white, Glenville) classroom, students challenged her reading of the TRC. Why students in this classroom objected is unclear. Ms. Prescott only taught one Grade 9 class, and, although neither school officially tracked students, her class was known as "the clever class." This coding may have given students the confidence to challenge their teacher. Regardless of the reason for their willingness to be outspoken, students' pushback in Ms. Prescott's class highlighted her desire to impart a story of moral equivalence. Her students' refusal to accept this narrative exasperated her to the point of telling them that they were "messed up in [the] head."

Ms. Prescott began by proposing two scenarios. In the first, a member of the apartheid regime killed someone. In the second, a member of a resistance movement killed someone. Ms. Prescott asked: "should [they] get the same punishment or different ones?" Lizzie, a biracial student, answered that "it depends on the justification around why [they] did the crime."

Ms. Prescott rejected Lizzy's view, saying: "Listen to the words that are coming out of your mouth! That's bull crap." Lizzie countered that "by killing, [the resister] brought change around. He ended apartheid." Ms. Prescott seemed genuinely frustrated and said: "Oh my soul! So, you are saying it's okay to kill? Oh, so now we get to different degrees of killing? So, if

EQUIVALENCES

I kill the little old lady who was irritating me versus one that stole from me, it's okay? Oh, my lord!"

Ravi, an Indian student, jumped to Lizzie's defense and said that the resistance fighter killed "to gain his freedom." Another student agreed and stated that the resister "did it in order to support his movement," and because "he's being oppressed."

Ms. Prescott made it clear that she disagreed and said "just because he's oppressed does not give him the right to kill. Killing is not the right way to go about it. . . . This is ridiculous. Killing is killing. You people are messed up in your head."

Students continued to challenge Ms. Prescott, now pointing out that all killing is *not* the same because people sometimes kill in self-defense. Several of the students argued that members of the resistance organization were acting in self-defense.

At that point, Ms. Prescott closed down the discussion. She concluded by telling students firmly that the resistance fighter was "not acting in self-defense. He's acting for political reasons. If [the member of the apartheid regime has] to be held accountable for killing as part of a political war then so should [the member of the resistance movement]."

She discredited the students' debate by suggesting that they were not thinking about this "logically" and that they were merely being contrarian to annoy her: "Logically think about it," she said. "You guys are just trying to piss me off now."

By focusing on violent resistance, teachers drew on the TRC's narrative of moral equivalence between white perpetrators and black resisters. This narrative displaces the racialized coding of victims and perpetrators. It also helps construct grand narratives around racial reconciliation in which the new, united polity is contrasted to the old regime in which different individuals acted badly toward each other.

A quote by Sibongile, an African student in the post-sample at Glenville, exemplifies this point. Halfway through my interviews with students, I transitioned from asking them about contemporary social issues to discussing their country's apartheid past. Drawing on methodology advanced by Howard Schuman and colleagues,[10] I began by asking students what they considered to be the most important event, and whom they considered to be the most important person, in South African history. Nearly 90 percent (89.6) named Nelson Mandela as the most important person:

> CHANA: Who would you say was the most important person in South African history?
> SIBONGILE: Mandela obviously.
> CHANA: Why?
> SIBONGILE: Because like he was able to forgive and put his life on hold for everyone.
> CHANA: Okay. Who did he forgive?
> SIBONGILE: Like everyone for the commotion that was caused—because I can't only say white people were the cause of everything . . . so I think he forgave everyone who was part of it.

For Sibongile and other students, Mandela is hailed for having forgiven, not whites, but "everyone who was part of it." Apartheid, in this understanding, was a conflict between two sides that—to quote Ms. Prescott—were involved "in a political war" and in which both did wrong. In teaching about apartheid, educators suggested that it is difficult to know on which "side of the story" individual actors may have been based solely on their race.

The purpose of learning apartheid, as Ms. Mokoena (African, Glenville)—quoted at the beginning of this chapter—explained, is not to create divisions between "us" and "them." Instead, the salient boundary becomes between "then" and "now." Njabulo, an African student in the post-sample at Roxbridge, summarized this aspect of *both sides of the story* when he answered my question about who was victimized or oppressed during apartheid: "Every race, even whites were a bit because blacks would also come and they'd hurt white people just because they couldn't get the things white people had. So, . . . it affected both sides."

WHAT WERE TEACHERS SO WORRIED ABOUT?

Why did *both sides of the story* form such a focal part of the teaching of apartheid? History teachers often remind us that the past is never over and gone, but lives on in the present. They tend to argue that we must learn the lessons of history or we are doomed to repeat them. But my observations and interviews saw teachers trying to decouple the past and the present, to disrupt continuity in order to stave off discomfort and conflict in their classrooms. Specifically, teachers used *both sides of the story* to assuage white students' feelings of guilt and delegitimize black students' claims about historical and contemporary racism.

EQUIVALENCES

Taryn, a white student who sat at the back of Ms. Devin's class at Roxbridge, raised her hand in class one day—the only time I heard this student speak during my observations. She said: "It almost makes you feel ashamed of being white when you hear this." This was not the type of comment students usually made, and I listened carefully for the teacher's response. Identifying with her student as a white South African, Ms. Devin answered by way of a story from her own high school days, shortly after the country's transition from apartheid to democracy:

> It is tough and, when I was in school and we studied apartheid, I felt really bad about what white people did to black people—*and I wasn't even there*. And one of my good friends was not white and I felt really uncomfortable sitting next to her in the lesson. But you have to remember, it was years ago and people were brought up years ago and they believed different things and *they weren't as educated as us*. Remember in 1948 there was not even TV. So now we're exposed to a whole lot of different cultures. But if you feel uncomfortable during the lessons please come tell me and I'll try [to] change my lessons so you don't feel uncomfortable. Remember, *none of us should feel uncomfortable 'cause none of us did it.* (emphasis added)

Ms. Devin was clearly concerned that her student felt ashamed because of her race.[11] She responded by assuring the whole class that apartheid had nothing to do with them—*we were not there, none of us did it*, and *they weren't as educated as us*.

As Ms. Devin finished speaking, Andrea, another white student, drew the conversation's focus to the first prong of the "both sides" rhetoric. She said: "Ma'am, there were also a lot of white people who fought against it." Ms. Devin agreed with Andrea and shared, "My grandpa got arrested. So, there were white people." Ms. Devin then contrasted her grandfather to her mother. "When I think of a bystander," she explained, "I think of my mom. . . . And I remember, I spoke to my mom once about it and she said she didn't know what was going on. And I said: 'How is that possible?' And she said it was not in the newspapers, her family shielded her."

Ms. Devin's interventions silenced an interrogation of the contemporary effects of apartheid in several ways. First, in emphasizing that many whites did not know, she focused on bystanders rather than beneficiaries and thus sidelined discussions of the contemporary racialized effects of apartheid. Second, in telling her students that "none of us did it," she distanced herself and them from the historical actors who perpetrated (rather than benefited from) apartheid crimes.[12] Finally, in focusing on individuals, she hindered her students from understanding the nature of structural racism—both past and present.

While teachers worried about making white students feel guilty, they seemed especially preoccupied with making sure that black students knew they were not the ones who suffered under apartheid—and that they should therefore not use apartheid, in the words of Ms. Devin, "as an excuse." Ms. Viljoen at Roxbridge, for example, explained how learning about apartheid could cause black students to focus on collective notions of suffering and the redress that these might entail. If the apartheid section is "not taught correctly," she explained in our interview, "it can lead to more division because you can have that whole idea of 'but that's how much we suffered' and 'I should get this.' But if it's taught correctly, it should not do that; it should do the opposite."

Similarly, when I asked Ms. Mokoena, the black African teacher quoted at the start of this chapter about the one or two things she hoped students would take away with them from learning the apartheid section, she drew on tropes of individualism and hard work to delegitimize black students' claims about the continued relevance of the past: "I'd hope that they learnt that hard work will get them through life. That they should stop sitting down and blaming somebody for the wrongs that were done in the past. They should get on with it and make something out of their lives; black, white, or Indian, it doesn't matter."

Ms. Devin, the Roxbridge teacher whose student, Taryn, expressed her white guilt, was similarly adamant that blacks should not focus on the past. In our interview, Ms. Devin explained, "I think that a lot of the white kids feel quite guilty about what happened and they're more sympathetic and empathetic about it because they think, 'Oh, it was me, like, I'm responsible.'" Without indicating that she had moved from thinking about her white students to contemplating her black students, Ms. Devin continued: "But I think in the two history classes I've taught, I think people dealt with it very maturely and no one used it as an excuse."

I wasn't sure what she meant, so I followed up and asked her what it would look like if a student "used it as an excuse."

Drawing on an example from her coaching role at the school, Ms. Devin responded, "We've had issues on the netball court,"[13] where, she said, some students would "be like, '*Ja* Ma'am, you know what you white people used to do to us black people,' blah-blah-blah."

Then, Ms. Devin seemed to get more specific, recounting a particular memory: "She said to us, 'Oh, it's just because I'm black.' I just turned around and was like, 'Actually, you don't know what you're talking about. You may know a little bit about it but you have no right to claim what happened because you didn't go through it. It's not your hurt that you're carrying.'"

In reflecting on the effects of apartheid history education on her students, Ms. Devin homed in on white guilt—but she quickly connected it to black students using apartheid "as an excuse." The "excuse," as she explained it, seemed to boil down to accusations that black students might make about racism at school. In managing such allegations on the sports fields, Ms. Devin discredited the students' claims by arguing, first, that black students have no right to make claims based on apartheid and, second, that their contemporary experiences of racism are illegitimate because they are based on historical claims. She tried to manage the potentially conflictual situation by distancing the past from students' current situations. In contrast, in her history classrooms, she told me, black students "dealt with it very maturely" and did not use apartheid "as an excuse." My classroom observations show how *both sides of the story* may have played a part in fostering this dynamic.

MANAGING CLASSROOM DYNAMICS

After completing my fieldwork at Glenville and Roxbridge, I conducted supplementary observations at a university seminar for postgraduate students who were working toward teaching diplomas. These observations allowed me to triangulate my findings. The postgraduate students I observed were learning how to teach the TRC section in schools.[14] The lecturer, a white woman, had just closed her introductory remarks when Luke, an African postgrad, asked how he was supposed to teach his own students that the TRC had "dealt with the past" when they were living in poverty in the present. Tossing out the name of an affluent area of Johannesburg, he said, "We haven't all moved to Sandton" and added, "these kids are not dumb. They know what's going on."

The lecturer answered that the Reconstruction and Development Programme (RDP) was supposed to deal with the economic aspects of apartheid.[15] Luke responded indignantly, "A four-walled box? With no amenities nearby?"[16] Another African student, Themba, jumped in: "The TRC looked at crimes committed within a bigger crime. It let whites live comfortably with the past while blacks have to live in the present where they are blamed for their own conditions. You know, we're still literally living in concentration camps down the road. And let me tell you, it's not good in the hood."

At that point, a white student named Mike joined in to respond to Luke and Themba, telling a story from a political science tutorial he attended as an undergraduate. There, a student asked why whites still have all the benefits. The tutor responded, "because Nelson Mandela sold you and me out."[17] Mike continued: "Well, I thought, 'Okay, *ja*, but that's kind of simplistic.' At what point do you stop blaming the past and also look at the present?" Referring to one of the articles that had been assigned to students in the seminar, Mike continued: "In that article we read, it says that the children and grandchildren and grandchildren's grandchildren have to apologize—." But before he could complete his sentence, the lecturer cut Mike and the conversation off. "Okay stop," she said. "Now we are getting to the readings, and I want to do the academic controversy exercise."

Students obliged, breaking into discussion groups, and I asked to join Luke's. As the discussion got under way, Luke turned to me and said, "You know, going back to your research topic, this is very difficult to teach in multiracial classrooms." He said that, especially as a black teacher, he feels that white students anticipate that he will make them feel guilty. I asked how he would respond if one of his students raised the points he'd raised earlier—that students, especially black students, know that racism is not a thing of the past and that the harms of apartheid had not been sufficiently redressed. He said, "It is very, very difficult." After a few moments' thought, Luke used the words that defined the way I saw apartheid taught in Roxbridge and Glenville's Grade 9 classes. "I think in teaching this history, it would be important to explain *both sides of the story*, to show that not all whites supported the system and that there were blacks who actually did support the system and worked with the government [emphasis added]."

These interactions highlight the process that Luke went through in realizing that telling *both sides of the story* is a way to minimize conflict and emotions such as guilt and anger in the classroom, including feelings directed at him—the teacher. Luke himself does not necessarily believe these things. When he was in his role as student, he—with Themba—focused on beneficiaries and the systemic violence of apartheid. As he transitioned to imagining his role as a teacher, Luke's focus shifted to individuals and the choices they made. He came to the realization that he could minimize the potential for conflict in his classroom by highlighting individual agency and complicating the racialized coding of victims and perpetrators. In so doing, he echoed the narratives of the TRC, which he had strongly criticized at the beginning of the class.

It is easy to judge the teachers at Glenville and Roxbridge High. Luke shows us that there is something more systemic going on. First, he exemplifies how imperatives around limiting the potential for conflict are a function of social roles, specifically tied to the social role of "teacher." Second, Luke seems to believe that there is a narrative that he is "supposed to tell." He seemed genuinely concerned at the beginning of the seminar when he asked the lecturer how he was supposed to teach his students that the TRC had adequately dealt with the past. No one in the room challenged the assumption that he had to. Finally, in drawing on narratives that are so similar to those articulated during the TRC, Luke and other teachers in this study show us that narratives of equivalence do not emerge out of thin air in schools and classrooms. Instead, they form part of what the sociologist Ann Swidler has called the "cultural toolkit" from which individuals draw to solve micro-interactional problems in the present.[18] The particular dynamics that pushed teachers to deploy *both sides of the story* may be specific to their schools and classrooms—but the narrative itself is part of the South African nation-building myth.

■ ■ ■

This chapter focused on how narratives of equivalence distanced the past from students' lived realities. By telling *both sides of the story*, teachers displaced the racialized coding of victims and perpetrators. Students were taught that one cannot know what "side of the story" historical actors were on simply by looking at their race. This, in turn, made it difficult for students to express, and identify with, historical and collective notions of guilt and victimization. In addition, by sidelining discussions of beneficiaries and focusing on extreme forms of political violence—rather than on racialized structures of inequality—teachers limited the validity of black students' claims about the socioeconomic effects of apartheid and contemporary instantiations of racism.

Teachers used *both sides of the story* to minimize animosities among students themselves, as well as between students and teachers. In their role as managers of classroom dynamics, they drew on narratives that were very similar to those articulated by the TRC. These narratives—which helped policymakers keep order at the macrosocial level during the transition to democracy—now provide a useful tool for teachers looking to keep order in the microsocial context of their schools and classrooms.

Teachers' motivations may not have been to reproduce racial hierarchies. However, by discrediting black students' experiences of racism and by teaching them that discussions of the legacies of the past are illegitimate, teachers reinforced the status quo in which white privilege becomes invisible; individual hard work becomes paramount; and blacks are forced to ensure that whites feel comfortable.

Thus far, I have looked at two mechanisms by which teachers charged with imparting the history of South African apartheid distanced the past: juxtapositions (specifically between apartheid and the Holocaust) and equivalences (between black and white suffering and between apartheid's enforcers and resisters). Before discussing the implications of these lessons for students' understandings of contemporary interpersonal and structural racism, I turn to a third distancing mechanism: experiential learning in the form of classroom simulations.

Chapter Four

SIMULATIONS

"**WHITES FIRST.** Blacks last," repeated the teachers as students filed into their classrooms and found their way to their racially segregated rows. It was a scene that only took place at Glenville High, where the educators argued that role-playing and simulations of apartheid-era segregation helped their ninth-graders build historical empathy. And it was a scene that only took place in the apartheid section of the curriculum: no other history lesson prompted Glenville's teachers to design historical simulations.

However enlivening these exercises might have been, my observations and interviews with students at both Glenville and Roxbridge revealed no pedagogical advantage to role-playing apartheid. Where the role-playing may have prompted educators to flesh out the social construction of race or its enduring effects in present-day South African life, it seemed instead to serve the purpose of distancing the past. To role-play history both minimized the brutality and bureaucracy of state-sanctioned racial segregation *and* served to frame apartheid as a discrete historical period, a vignette unconnected to events before or after, or a system with no legacy. The combined effect was a stifling of potentially productive conversation and, of course, potential conflict.

GLENVILLE'S "ZULU CLASSES" AND "AFRIKAANS CLASSES"

At Glenville High, a unique process allocates students to classrooms, resulting in some racially diverse classrooms and some populated only by black African students. The system, unsurprisingly, had implications for how the apartheid simulations played out in different teachers' history classes.

South African high school students are required to take two languages as school subjects—one at "first language" level and the other at "second language" level—and every student at Glenville and Roxbridge took English as their first language. Roxbridge offered just one second-language option, Afrikaans, while Glenville allowed students to choose between Afrikaans and isiZulu. In practice, only black African students chose isiZulu as their second language. Other students told me that they had considered choosing isiZulu but were told that they would require "first language" proficiency to keep up with the lessons. Dissuaded, they took Afrikaans instead.[1]

These decisions were not trivial. At Glenville, students were sorted into classrooms based on their choice of second language.

So, students who chose isiZulu as their second language also took *every* other school subject with fellow isiZulu students, and students who chose Afrikaans learned alongside their fellow Afrikaans students. Although each of the Grade 9 classes was assigned a letter (grade 9A through grade 9I), informally, Glenville's students and teachers alike spoke about the "Afrikaans classes" and the "Zulu classes." While the six "Afrikaans classes" were racially diverse, the three "Zulu classes" were composed entirely of black African students.

"WHITES FIRST"

The apartheid section lasted two and a half months. For ten weeks, Grade 9 students had to enter Ms. Prescott (white) and Ms. Ndlovu's (African) multiracial classrooms by race and sit in rows segregated by race. Lining up outside their classrooms before each period was nothing new—it happens every day in most South African schools, and I saw it at Roxbridge too. There, students would wait in two neat rows on opposite sides of the corridor—boys on one side, girls on the other. When signaled by the teachers, the girls would enter the room first, boys next. The process of walking into class allowed teachers to check for uniform infractions: boys whose hair was too long or girls whose hair was not adequately tied back, untucked shirts, makeup, or unsanctioned jewelry (usually anything but a small religious symbol and/or one stud in each ear for girls). At Roxbridge, it was not uncommon for the class to start with boys being sent up to the office to shave, girls being sent to the bathroom to wash makeup off their faces, and—on occasion—demerits being given. But, at Glenville, I watched Ms. Prescott and Ms. Ndlovu stand at the doors of their racially diverse "Afrikaans classes," directing students to enter "Whites first. Blacks last" and present their "passbook" as they went.[2]

Under the apartheid policy of "influx control," which aimed to regulate black urbanization, the passbook (alternatively known as the "dompas" or the "pass") served as an internal passport that demarcated whether, and for how long, its bearer could move within urban areas. All African males over the age of sixteen (females were added later) were required to carry these notorious identification documents, which featured a photograph, identifying information, any arrest records, and employment history. (Indians and Coloureds had identity documents that stipulated their race, but the terms "dompas" and "passbook" referred to the documents carried by Africans.) In the *simulated* apartheid of their classrooms, African, Coloured, and Indian students were all required to carry a "passbook" to gain entry to their classroom. White students were exempt.

In Ms. Prescott's classroom, students were required to make their own passbooks, but they received minimal instruction regarding how the passbooks should look or what they should contain (resulting in some "passbooks" that were just scribbles on a piece of paper). Ms. Ndlovu, however, told her students to carry a photocopy of a real identity document. She explained the rules: "Everyone is going to have a pass. I won't require original documents, but you must photocopy a birth certificate or a passport or an ID book and I will not allow you into class without a pass." For several days, one student brought her actual passport to school, using it to gain entry to her history classroom. Ms. Ndlovu also suggested that the passbooks must be shown upon demand, regardless of whether students were in history class or even on the school grounds:

> So, this pass system is not only for entrance. If I see you by the [sports] courts, I will ask for a pass and I want you to produce that pass. If you don't have it, you will get a fine or go to jail. The reason is that they were supposed to move with that document from place to place. They were supposed to have it all the time, even when they were sleeping—so if the police comes to their house and says "dompas," they have to produce it. If I see you at [the shopping mall] during the week [and] you are wearing a school uniform, I want a pass. If it is on the weekend, I won't [ask for it].

Because none of the students ever mentioned being asked for their passbooks outside of her classroom, I suspect Ms. Ndlovu never made good on this threat. But having the weekend off was just one example of the disjuncture between real and simulated apartheid.

Once in the classroom, students sat in rows segregated by race. They exited the classroom—as they had entered it—by race. The punishments for forgetting to carry a passbook, as Ms. Ndlovu indicated, were typically "paying a fine" or "going to jail." The former entailed giving the teacher either five South African Rands—about sixty cents in USD at the time—or canned food at the next class. The latter meant sitting on the floor at the front of a different history teacher's classroom. On at least one occasion, Ms. Ndlovu made a group of students who did not bring their passbooks sit outside, on the floor, in the cold school corridor.

APARTHEID WITHOUT WHITES

Ms. Mokoena, an African teacher who led one of the "Afrikaans classes," also segregated her classroom and had her students carry "passes" for the duration of the apartheid section. It happened that her class had no white students, and so her simulation put Indian students to one side of the room, African students to the other, and Coloured students in the middle.

In Ms. Ndlovu's pair of "Zulu classes," she resolved the dilemma of reenacting apartheid in the absence of whites by segregating her students by ethnicity. She told the classes, "Zulus come in first because our president is Zulu. Then Sothos 'cause our deputy president is Sotho."[3] It was unclear to me how the rest of the classroom was organized. The only rule that seemed to be enforced was that Zulus entered first and sat in their own row.

As the simulation progressed, students in these classrooms began to regulate the ethnic boundaries Ms. Ndlovu set. My fieldnotes captured one such incident: "A male student starts walking into class, another male student pulls him back and says: 'This is apartheid! Zulus first. Who do you think you are?'"

Ms. Ndlovu did not use the simulation to explore the apartheid state's "divide and rule" policy in creating separate "homelands" for different African "tribes." None of the teachers interrogated the apartheid state's creation of a four-tiered (rather than, say, a two-tiered) racial hierarchy. Most striking, however, was how the simulated apartheid in these three classes obscured any understanding or engagement with the concept of white privilege. Black students who carried passes into their classrooms may have got a sense of how regulated life was for blacks under apartheid. But, in the absence of whites in the simulation, the idea of apartheid as a system that created and protected white privilege was lost.

POLICING THE RACIAL BOUNDARIES

Although Ms. Ndlovu, Ms. Prescott, and Ms. Mokoena allowed students to self-identify for the simulation, teachers used their own categorizations to manage their classrooms.[4] Ms. Prescott, in particular, regularly stood at the door to her classroom and called students by name if they did not enter with their presumed racial group.

Just as the students in Ms. Ndlovu's "Zulu classes" began to regulate ethnic boundaries among themselves, students in other classrooms took it upon themselves to police the racial boundaries. For example, when Naila, who had one Coloured parent and one Indian parent, chose the "Coloured row," an Indian student turned to her and asked, "Aren't you Indian? Come sit here." As Naila moved to his row, he joked, "I have transformed her!" Several days later, when Naila sat in the Coloured row again, an Indian student called her "a confused child." I was not immune to this racial regulation: When I sat at the back of the classroom in an open seat in the "Indian row," students asked Ms. Ndlovu to tell me that I was in the wrong group. Trying to minimize the impact of my presence on the research site, I smiled and quietly found myself a spot in the "white row."

In Ms. Mokoena's classroom, with its tripartite separation, an Indian male student asked about a fellow student: "Why is [she] sitting in the Indian group?" A classmate chimed in, "She's Indian," at which point the girl they were talking about corrected, "I'm mixed race." The male student responded, "She's a mongrel," but he was shut down by another student who interrupted, "No! Don't say that." Ms. Mokoena intervened. Commenting on the student in question, she settled the matter: "Because she looks more Indian and her name is Indian, she'd be sent to the Indian area."

Instead of addressing the pejorative language used in her classroom ("she's a mongrel"), Ms. Mokoena took on the role of the apartheid state and categorized her student racially. In doing so (and as I discuss more soon), she missed the opportunity to explore the social construction of race and the very real consequences of such social constructions.

Ms. Mokoena herself used racial slurs constantly throughout the apartheid section, referring to her Indian students as "coolies," her African students as "natives," and blacks in general as "darkies." At one point, a student reading aloud her answer to a class activity referred to blacks as "darkies." Ms. Mokoena interjected, "Don't say darkies. That's my slang." In the next lesson, Ms. Mokoena reminded her students: "Don't write 'darkies' in your test." A student asked what would happen if they did; Ms. Mokoena responded that she would "mark it wrong." When an

Indian female student suggested, "Just write pickaninnies," Ms. Mokoena did not respond. In this classroom, where there were no whites, all students were subjected to similar treatment by Ms. Mokoena, and students themselves began to throw around racially offensive language as freely as Ms. Mokoena did.

Like Ms. Mokoena, Ms. Prescott implicitly took on the role of the apartheid state at various points in the simulation. For example, when an African student brought a tin of pilchards to "pay a fine" (this time, for doing poorly on a test rather than forgetting a passbook), Ms. Prescott asked her students in a bantering tone, "Do you guys eat this at home? It's homeland food!"[5] All the students laughed along, and she continued with her lesson. On another occasion, Ms. Prescott stood at the door, letting students in by race, and took on the same kind of jesting tone to address her African students: "Black people, why are you always standing up front when you know you come in last? You must know your place." On another day, as her students fumbled for their passbooks in their bags, she prodded the African students by commenting loudly, "You are proving my point." "What is your point?" asked one of the students, to which she clarified bluntly, "That black people are incompetent."

It is perhaps surprising that black students played along in this multiracial classroom. Instead, classroom relations appeared to remain friendly, even as Ms. Prescott humiliated and berated her black students. As I've reported in other work, black students in both schools were frequently pushed to interpret racially charged incidents as "only jokes."[6] This broader context likely played into the jovial atmosphere in Ms. Prescott's classroom. Another important factor in this puzzling calm is that the three white students in Ms. Prescott's Grade 9 classroom were exceptionally well-liked and socially integrated within racially diverse groups of friends. When I walked through the school during recess, I often saw small groups of white students sitting together. But the three white students in Ms. Prescott's class were not part of them. Instead, they socialized in racially diverse groups of friends. In interviews, when I asked students to name their two or three closest friends, all three named—and were named by—black students.

One could imagine a less friendly atmosphere in the simulated apartheid if the white students had regularly kept to themselves. Instead, black and white students in Ms. Prescott's classroom maintained their good relations while agreeing to "play along" in the simulation. This dynamic was succinctly demonstrated one day while students waited for Ms. Prescott to arrive and check their passes. Thandi, an African student from a different classroom, went into Ms. Prescott's room to retrieve something she had forgotten, prompting James, one of the white students, to caution her: "Don't let Ms. Prescott see you." Thandi turned to hug James hello, asking, "Why not?" James, arms around her, replied: "Cause we are doing apartheid now."

Aside from being segregated and having to carry passes, the students in Ms. Ndlovu's classroom were spared the differential treatment and racist language of her colleagues' classrooms. As I entered her classroom one day, walking behind a white student, Ms. Ndlovu told me that it was okay if I went in, but the student needed to show a pass "because other students were complaining." Sensitive to students' claims of unfairness, Ms. Ndlovu continued the simulation but extended the pass system to whites. As in her "Zulu classes," the dimension of white privilege became invisible in the simulation performed in her multiracial "Afrikaans classes."

"TESTING THE BOUNDARIES"

Only in Ms. Prescott's classroom was white privilege explicitly explored. A series of exchanges that unfolded over several days brought this topic to the fore. These began when Nathan, a white student, asked in reference to a famous white anti-apartheid activist, "If one of us blokes wants to be Helen Joseph, do we face the same penalties?"[7] Ms. Prescott responded with a simple "yes." Nathan pushed on, "Well, if we are the Helen Josephs, then can we integrate with the people of color?" Ms. Prescott came quite close to outlining a particular challenge of ally activism with her reply, saying: "Yes, let me tell you about that. Many people of color said it was very good for Beyers Naudé and Helen Joseph to stand in Parliament and protest but, at the end of the day, they still go back to the white areas. So, they can get up and protest, but at the end of the day, they still go back to their suburban houses and the best life can offer . . . they still get the privileges of being white." Then she warned the would-be protestors, "So, you are more than welcome—but in my context, you will not get the same privileges."

Nathan then asked: "So, am I betraying you?" At this point, James, the other white student in the class, interjected: "What are you saying, man?" Ms. Prescott told them, "Look, the punishment will be worse for all of you." One of the Coloured students motioned to Nathan, saying, "Come here, Nathan. We'll make room for you." Ms. Prescott was already moving on with her lesson plan as another Coloured student countered, "We don't need your help."

The next day, I walked into the classroom and noticed Nathan sitting in the African row. Ms. Prescott inquired, "What are you doing on this side of the room?" as a black student exclaimed, "Nathan, you freedom fighter!" Amid laughter, Nathan got up and found a seat in the white row. On August 10, the day after South Africans celebrated National Women's Day in honor of the 1956 Women's March, Nathan once again looked like he was heading for the African row when Ms. Prescott addressed him: "If you are Helen Joseph today, then you have to be Helen Joseph every day. You don't choose when you are going to be an activist." Nathan explained, "Just for Women's Rights Day yesterday," but Ms. Prescott responded with a simple "No," and Nathan sat with the other white students.

A few days later, as Ms. Prescott called the white students to enter the class, Nathan ignored the directive. "Is this your day to resist, Nathan?" his teacher asked him, and when he responded affirmatively, she prodded, "Are you *sure*?" Nathan shook his head, indicating that he was not, in fact, sure. "So, come," said Ms. Prescott as she gestured him to enter. An African student interjected: "Go *baas*."[8] At that point, Nathan declared, "I have to start a revolution." A black student put his arm around Nathan and said, "You're one of us now," as they entered the classroom together.

Once all students were seated, Madison, the only white girl in the class, pointed to the African students' section and asked, "Why is Nathan sitting there?"

"He's resisting," Ms. Prescott said.

"Resisting what?" Madison pushed.

"I don't know," answered Ms. Prescott.

At that, Madison got up and moved to the Coloured row. "I also want to resist," she said.

"Madison, you're an embarrassment to the white people," Ms. Prescott began, adding, "James is the only true one here." As Nathan shouted out, "Helen Joseph!" Madison retorted, "Ma'am, it's boring to be white."

"How is it boring?" asked Ms. Prescott, pointing to the black African students. "They're an oppressed nation. They have no resources. They have nothing."

Madison, who by this time had gone back to the white row, murmured, "They have each other."

From then on, Nathan entered class with the African students. Though his teacher frequently joked that she was going to "put him in jail for torture" and give him "a detention as torture for defying [her]," I never saw the student formally punished. Instead, his repeated challenges were counter-challenged with vague threats. At one point, Ms. Prescott asked him: "Are you sure you want to defy me?"

"What," Nathan wondered, "are the consequences?"

Rather than answer directly, Ms. Prescott asked only: "Are you *sure*?"

As if in a standoff, Nathan indicated his concern with another query, "Will I regret it ma'am?" It seemed to me that Nathan was challenging the rules but also wanted assurance that, within the simulation and the classroom in general, the penalties for his pushback would not be severe.

SIMULATIONS

At no other point did I see students challenge the simulations so explicitly. Ms. Prescott later told me that "there's never been anybody else. [Nathan] is the first" to have pushed back this way in all her years of teaching this history. Further, she noted, neither of the other white students in this classroom, Madison or James, had decided to "test the boundaries" like Nathan. She speculated, "I don't think that they realized that they could have. [Nathan] did, but [Nathan] only went as far as to jump ship and go to the other side. He didn't realize he could've—well, all of them didn't realize—he could've staged an uprising or tried to overthrow me because I'm just one person, you know. But *ja* [yes], he was quite perturbed by [the simulation]."

I asked why the teacher thought Nathan had acted differently from her other students over the years. Ms. Prescott pointed to his family and friends. "His parents," she told me, are "very liberal people," and his "best friend is a black guy." Ms. Prescott continued: "He's been brought up in a multiracial, multicultural [environment] and I think he felt the effects of just being the white guy when all his friends were on that side [of the classroom]. So, I think in solidarity to his friends, he decided to go the other route. *Ja*, I think that's ultimately it—for his friends."

Certainly, the insight that Nathan's family is very liberal might explain his familiarity with the white anti-apartheid activist Helen Joseph. Still, Ms. Prescott returned to the idea that Nathan was motivated by his loyalties to his friends. That, too, made some sense, given that Madison, finding herself alone—the only girl in the white row while her friends "had each other" in another section—considered (but eventually backed away from) a direct "test" of Ms. Prescott's authority.

Recall that Ms. Prescott had evoked the names of prominent white anti-apartheid activists, while minimizing both the impact and personal effects of their resistance. Many blacks, she told the students, said it was good and well for whites to "go to Parliament and protest," but they ultimately went back to their white neighborhoods, where they continued to enjoy their privileges. It struck me that this statement countered the "both sides of the story" narrative—that both black and white people suffered harm because of apartheid. It also glossed over the real sacrifices made by whites who joined resistance movements. Beyers Naudé, for example, was declared a "banned person" and put under house arrest for seven years, during which time he was not allowed to be in a room with more than one other person at a time. Helen Joseph was charged with high treason and also declared a "banned person." She survived several assassination attempts.[9]

It is true that these individuals continued to benefit from whiteness, even as they resisted white supremacy. But to suggest that they (and others like them) continued to enjoy the same privileges as whites who did not join the resistance minimizes the contributions of these "struggle heroes," as they are referred to in South Africa. Whereas the "both sides of the story" narrative, highlighted in the previous chapter, equated black oppression under apartheid with whites' inability to interact socially with blacks, this rhetorical shift dismissed the price paid by whites who put themselves on the line in the struggle against apartheid.

The role of white allies is not only something that was hotly debated among the different anti-apartheid resistance movements but is also an important question in contemporary antiracist struggles. Ms. Prescott did not explore any of these issues. Instead, she dismissed the notion of white resistance during apartheid, at the same time threatening harsh penalties for such resistance in her classroom's simulation. Had she actually meted out such penalties, it would have presented another useful opening for a discussion of the reasons that some whites joined the resistance while most did not. Neither in the formal curriculum nor in Glenville's simulation exercises were such conversations fostered; Nathan's act of defiance was instead dismissed as an example of "testing the boundaries" and pushing to sit with his friends.

Ms. Prescott's comment that none of the students realized they could have "staged an uprising" stuck out to me. I can't but wonder what would have happened if the students *had* attempted an uprising, challenging the simulation not by playing the role of apartheid-era resisters, but from their own positions as racialized subjects in a post-apartheid classroom reenacting a brutal past that affects their everyday lives. When Nathan's actions presented a perfect opportunity to explore white privilege and the costs of white resistance, they were instead transformed into a joking exchange, neutralized by the teacher's response. Rajesh, an Indian student, recalled in our interview that Nathan had pushed back as "a joke because him and Ms. Prescott are friends." When Madison asked what exactly Nathan was protesting, it's no wonder Ms. Prescott stepped in to answer, "I don't know."

SIMULATIONS

WHAT DID TEACHERS HOPE TO ACHIEVE?

I tried to find out how the Glenville teachers had come up with the idea of the simulations as well as what they hoped to achieve by implementing experiential learning in just this one module of the Grade 9 history curriculum. Ms. Prescott, the head of Glenville's history department, told me that, far from being an organized effort, the apartheid simulation idea had just come to her. Other teachers picked it up from there, making it an informal tradition over time. No one was trained to run the simulation or debriefed at its end—in fact, the simulation simply dropped off when the apartheid section was finished and teachers informed students that they could sit wherever they pleased.

At first, Ms. Prescott said, the apartheid simulation was just a one-week exercise, but over the years she made it longer and longer. "The ultimate thing," she explained, "was for them to experience what it ultimately feels like to be constantly checked up on and to have some stupid piece of paper or document that identifies you." She told me she thought the simulation could help students "put [themselves] in somebody else's shoes" so that they could "empathize or sympathize" with historical others "because they [students] obviously have never been brought up in that—where they've been checked and questioned and, you know, discriminated [against] because of the color of their skin." Ms. Mokoena similarly described the simulation as just a "little taste of what it must've been like in the apartheid system," with teachers "making sure that they [students] are able to feel exactly how it must have been like." And Ms. Ndlovu understood it as an exercise in building historical perspective. "In history," she told me, "you have to empathize . . . it was a skill which we were teaching them."

"This is very unique to the apartheid section," Ms. Prescott responded when I asked about integrating this type of experiential learning into the other history sections. She explained, "This is the only time I do an activity like this because [of] the division of the races." But then she thought about another section dealing with racial segregation: the civil rights movement in the United States. She clarified: "I don't do it when I'm teaching the civil rights movement because I don't think it's beneficial because that's an American part of history. So, to the children, it wouldn't mean anything. I think it works more—this works better because it's our history."

The idea that teachers did not employ experiential learning when exploring historical events in other places because "it wouldn't mean anything" to students is a curious one. If the purpose of experiential learning is to collapse space and time, giving people access to the experiences of historical actors, then distant histories would arguably be the optimal lessons for such activities. And if apartheid is something close, something to which students can relate, then perhaps a more instructive exercise would have explored students' own lived experiences. In an odd way, then, the extended apartheid role-playing helped reinforce the overarching message: that the recent apartheid past was *actually* very much past, accessible only through a simulation. In Ms. Prescott's understanding, the simulation gave students a sense of apartheid that they would not otherwise have "because they obviously have never been . . . discriminated [against] because of the color of their skin." So, while the purpose of the simulation might have been to enhance empathy, the message was also that segregation and discrimination are not things students know about, that these are distant things in the country's past that can only be experienced by "stepping into someone else's shoes."[10]

WHAT DID STUDENTS LEARN?

Just one student in my post-sample interviews at Glenville problematized the ten-week apartheid activity, suggesting it reinforced racial divisions. Most students recommended that teachers continue using the activity in future years, saying it was good and gave them a sense of what apartheid must have been like. Leela, an Indian student in Ms. Ndlovu's class, explained, "We lived the life, so we knew exactly what was going on and how it felt."

Those students who did not like the activity said that carrying the pass was a nuisance and the simulation prevented them from sitting with their friends. Take, for instance, my conversation with an Indian student named Ishani. "Normally, when we sit in class, we're mixed up," Ishani described. "I'd have a black friend on this side and a white friend or an Indian friend next to me." The simulation, she explained, "actually made me feel how they felt then . . . being separated." Ishani said she "hated" the role-playing because she "couldn't talk to another race. . . . It was like only us Indians who could talk to each other and nobody else." And that, she insisted, was the whole point:

SIMULATIONS

"I think [the teacher] wanted us to know how it feels to like not talk to somebody from another race. She wants us to feel how they felt when it was apartheid." Sizwe, an African student in one of Ms. Ndlovu's "Zulu classes," had a similar appraisal: "I'm a different—from a different ethnic group from my friends," he told me, "so [the simulation] gave me a sort of view of like how people were segregated."

Only Kagiso, an African student in one of Ms. Ndlovu's classes, talked about the negative effects of simulating apartheid, especially how it reinforced and naturalized racial divisions between students. "I didn't really like it," she shared, "because, you know, it feels—because since that day, you know, 'til the last day of school, people have been sitting like that. No one changed back to their normal places. So, I feel that people are looking at that and actually feel comfortable with their own racial groups, instead of feeling uncomfortable and wanting to know more about others."

Most students, however, viewed the segregation of the simulation as something different—and distanced—from their daily lives. In focusing on limits placed on interaction across racial lines, students were able to contrast past to present. In interviews, when I asked students to imagine that they were living during apartheid and to think about how their lives might have been different, many—in both schools—mentioned that they would not have the friends they have now. Aiden, a Coloured student in the post-sample at Roxbridge, told me that his life would have been "a whole lot different" if he had lived during apartheid. He explained, "I wouldn't have a different race of friends, I wouldn't be learning in a classroom with different friends, I wouldn't be playing sport with my different races, I wouldn't be socializing with white people."

Similar ideas emerged when I asked students about their national identity. The vast majority described being South African as meaning that they came from a diverse country where they could interact and socialize across racial lines. The simulation reinforced this emphasis on apartheid as a system of social segregation, while downplaying the material dimensions of inequality that underpinned this segregation.

In addition to focusing on segregation, the simulation revolved around one of apartheid's most notorious laws: the Natives (Abolition of Passes and Coordination of Documents) Act of 1952 (commonly known as the Pass Laws Act).[11] Far from giving students a deeper understanding of the act's significance in regulating the lives of black Africans, the simulation trivialized its effects by constructing the carrying of passes as, at worst, a "nuisance"—or even "fun." Jalela, an Indian student, explained, "I thought it was fun . . . the white people had to enter first and like so on, so I thought it was kind of cool."

Kira, a biracial student at Glenville, laughed at first when I asked her what she thought of the passbooks activity. She then explained it to me as an annoyance: "Oh, it was really frustrating because there were a few times where I forgot mine, and it's like—it's just an unnecessary way of getting yourself in trouble. So, *ja*, I didn't like it." Nonetheless, she recommended that teachers do the activity the following year.

Ms. Prescott was aware of these as common responses, telling me that most students react predictably to the simulation. "In the beginning they find it to be a big joke. They find it hilarious." After a while, however, "they get annoyed with it, and they get irritated with it because they've got to remember it [the pass]." At times, Ms. Prescott confessed, she felt the same. "I also forget at times and don't want to do it either," she explained, "because it's such a *schlep*. It takes fifteen minutes of your life to check it [the passbook] or whatever the case."

The idea of the simulation as "fun" or "amusing" came to the fore in Ms. Ndlovu's classrooms, where, in addition to carrying passes and sitting in rows segregated by race, students reenacted the Defiance Campaign and the Women's March. The former was a campaign during which people deliberately defied apartheid laws. Part of the campaign entailed either burning one's passbook or leaving it at home. The Women's March—mentioned earlier in relation to Nathan's wish "to be Helen Joseph"—refers to the 1956 march by twenty thousand South African women to the state president's office in Pretoria to protest the pass laws.

In one of her racially diverse classrooms, Ms. Ndlovu called a white student named Benjamin to sit up front next to her. "We are now looking at the Defiance Campaign," she explained. "Benjamin is representing the white government." She framed the exercise with a short explanation, telling her students that the Defiance Campaign "happened in 1952 and the aim was to defy all the laws the apartheid government introduced." Then she instructed the students to leave the classroom and, when they reentered, to "approach Benjamin" and Jacob, another white male in the class, who "will be the police." They were to tell Benjamin and Jacob what they thought of the passbook system. To Benjamin and Jacob, she said, "You have to respond and say, 'We are not going to change that.'"

SIMULATIONS

Sitting at the teacher's desk, Benjamin watched as his classmates walked out, while Jacob picked up a broomstick and held it like a baton. As the students came back into the classroom, they approached the white students and said things like "I don't want inequality" and "I don't want unfairness." Ms. Ndlovu corrected them: "Remember, we are talking about *rules*." Trying again, a student urged Benjamin, "I don't want to walk around with my ID booklet everywhere. It's annoying!" Benjamin responded, "You must!" as another student shouted, "We want the right to vote!"

All this time, the mood remained light—to the point that Ms. Ndlovu asked with exasperation, "Why are you laughing?" as the students continued to lodge their complaints with the "white government." "This type of passport, I don't want it," said one. "No segregation, okay?" said another as the giggling and chatting continued. "You know what is amusing?" asked Ms. Ndlovu rhetorically, "You didn't even throw away your passes. You can't say 'I don't want a pass' when you have one. The whole idea is those people, they came and threw their passes." One of her students protested. "But tomorrow we'll need it and we won't have it," he said. "I said you'll get it back, didn't I?" exclaimed Ms. Ndlovu.

The issue of students needing their passes after the Defiance Campaign simulation came up in Ms. Ndlovu's other classroom as well. As Paul took on the role of the apartheid state, Ms. Ndlovu explained: "Paul will give you back your passes 'cause you will need them for the Sharpeville Massacre. There you will burn them." Ms. Ndlovu never did ask her students to reenact the Sharpeville Massacre, in which police opened fire and killed sixty-nine protestors, but her students kept their passes all the same.

SIMULATIONS

When it came time to learn about the Women's March, Ms. Ndlovu once more used role-playing. Summing up her students' performance, she again homed in on how they had not taken the activity seriously. "If I can comment on the presentation," she said, "it was very bad. You were not even serious. You were laughing. I don't think people would go to the authorities and laugh, 'Oh, we don't want passes.' They will not take you seriously."

Aside from the fact that students found the role-playing amusing, the activity undermined the idea that historical reenactments give one a sense of what it must have been like in the past. When students reacted to the simulation in the present (by saying that it would be bad to destroy their passbooks in the Defiance Campaign activity because they would need them later), Ms. Ndlovu did not take the opportunity to emphasize that, in the past they were ostensibly recreating, there would have been grave consequences for such protest participation.

What students learned from the simulation exercise was unclear to me. At Roxbridge High, the pass laws were also a big focus in the curriculum, but teachers took a different approach. Instead of reenacting the laws, students were asked to research and recreate a passbook, on which they were graded. The grading rubric used included points for effort and neatness as well as for historical accuracy. In my interviews with students, I asked them to list and explain apartheid's main laws. This was one of the main areas where I noticed differences between my pre- and post- samples, with students in the post-sample being able to list more laws than students in the pre-sample. While students in both schools frequently mentioned the pass laws, students at Roxbridge were much more likely than Glenville students to understand what the passbook contained, what purpose it served, and who had to carry it. I cannot make general claims about the effects of experiential learning on knowledge acquisition. I can, however, say that, in the case of Glenville High, the simulation did not lead to better informational outcomes than did the more traditional ways of learning adopted at Roxbridge High.

THE NONSIMULATORS

In the first lesson covering the apartheid section, Glenville's Mr. Pretorius (white) asked his students to move around so they were sitting in racially homogenous groups. Students continued sitting in this segregated manner throughout the section, but Mr. Pretorius did not actively enforce the practice. Mr. Lane (white) did not use role-playing in his teaching at all. I asked Ms. Prescott why some teachers conducted the simulation while others did not. She explained: "They can do it if they want to do it; they don't have to. We work on a basis of you obviously have your own—we're not conformed [*sic*] in terms of how we teach." Ms. Ndlovu told me that she thought that Mr. Pretorius and Mr. Lane didn't embrace the simulation because they were trained as geography teachers rather than as history teachers.[12] Additionally, Ms. Prescott's, Ms. Ndlovu's, and Ms. Mokoena's classrooms were all next to one another on the same corridor, so they could observe and get ideas from one another throughout the school year. Mr. Pretorius's and Mr. Lane's classrooms were in other parts of the school. This difference might explain why Mr. Pretorius did not implement the simulation in all its detail. But why didn't Mr. Lane implement it at all?

When I interviewed Mr. Lane, he told me that "the one teacher, [which] I thought was brilliant, you know, let the whites go in first and then the blacks went; which was the reality at the time and it's a good way of teaching it." In other words, Mr. Lane thought the simulation was a good teaching tool; he was simply unaware that it was being conducted, in some version or another, in every other Grade 9 history classroom in his school. Nonetheless, when I asked whether he would consider doing the simulation the following year, he answered negatively. He homed in on 9M—the "Zulu class" he taught—as he explained:

> MR. LANE: No, I wouldn't . . . No. Because then—maybe it ingrains—because a lot of these kids . . . especially that [9M] class . . . remember what [Victoria] said? Were you there that day? . . .You weren't there that day. [Victoria] said she grows up in an environment where the parents or the family is not prepared to do anything. They want the handout because they didn't have it in the '80s and the '90s. And you can't live like—well, for me, you can't live like that. That's why that [9M] is a product . . . It's an animal, you know. They're like a human being. Those fourteen kids are like one person. Because a lot of the parents in there are domestic workers, a lot of them are unemployed, a lot of them sit around and wait for this [to be given to them]—instead of—proactive is a big word,

but just go out and get a job. And they won't, you know. And [Victoria] laughs and smiles because I don't think she understands that you have a responsibility, you know. So it's very tough for them, especially those kids because [Mthembu's] mom is a maid, [Xolani's] mom's a maid. I think [Rebecca's] mom is a maid [pause]. [Sabelo's] mother, I don't think even works. Poverty! . . . I mean it's got nothing [to do] with this but, you know, that's the context that a lot of these kids [are] coming [from] . . . a lot of them know where they're going and a lot of them are still very, very lost and I think that might be because of the influence of their parents and their grandparents. . . . But all those things are going to impact on these kids at a certain level and then it's us against them, you know, it's us against them.

CHANA: In what way?

MR. LANE: The blacks against the whites. . . . You see, the thing is, if you take that into adulthood and you've got people like Julius Malema telling them that mines are [to be nationalized]—all those things that he says that are just absolutely irrational.[13] And then they go: "Hold on a second, but who owns the money? Oh, the stock exchange is owned by the white people, *ja*," you know . . . I'm making a lot of assumptions here but if they are told those sorts of things: "*Ja* the white—you know—who's the managing director of Anglo?[14] No, it's a white guy."

In this exchange, Mr. Lane initially declined to consider a simulation on the grounds that "maybe it ingrains." He didn't articulate *what* it "ingrains," but his thoughts shifted to his 9M class, known in the school as a "problem class." Indeed, on the first day of my fieldwork at Glenville, Ms. Prescott introduced me to the history teachers and told me that I would be observing all of their classrooms—except for 9M because it had "behavioral issues." I decided not to push the issue at that point, but asked if it would be all right to approach students from that class for interviews. Ms. Prescott agreed.

Later in the day, chatting with Mr. Lane in the staff room, I asked about 9M. He told me they were "very naughty" and that the "ringleader in the class" had stated that Julius Malema was her hero. I said the class sounded interesting and that I would be curious to sit in on his lessons, if he didn't mind. He said that it would be fine, but explained that the teaching team had initially thought that I should not observe that class so as to make sure I had "the best possible experience" at Glenville. I responded that I would still be observing all the other classes but, to get a full picture, it would be great if I could observe 9M too. Mr. Lane said that I could. Later, when I confirmed with Ms. Prescott, she also agreed.

So this was the background for Mr. Lane's seemingly tangential comment about declining to do a simulation in his 9M class. As he searched for a way to explain the potentially undesirable ideas the exercise could "ingrain," Mr. Lane started describing how students in 9M receive messages from home that prevent them from realizing the kind of individualistic achievement ideology promoted by teachers. These students—who all came from low-income backgrounds—were already beginning to listen to the rhetoric of Julius Malema.

SIMULATIONS

During my fieldwork, Malema was invoked in both schools as a proxy for irrational, vengeful discourses that fixate on the past. Malema was the president of the ANC Youth League until he was expelled from the party in 2012 (having lost an appeal of his 2011 suspension) on the grounds that he was sowing divisions within the organization. The previous year, he was found guilty of "hate speech" for inciting violence against white farmers. Around the time that my fieldwork was conducted, Malema, who advocates land restitution and nationalization of the mines, had been criticized extensively in the media for his lavish lifestyle. In the classrooms I observed, he was often the subject of jokes and ridicule.

And yet, even at that time, he had a considerable following—especially among economically marginalized young sectors of South Africa's population. Today, and as I discuss further in the conclusion, he is the leader of the Economic Freedom Fighters (EFF)—a political party established in 2013 that, within a year, became the third largest party in Parliament. In many ways, Malema's views represent a profound criticism of the ideology of rupture articulated in institutions such as the South African Truth and Reconciliation Commission (see chapter 1). Malema, essentially, suggests that white privilege continues unabated in the new dispensation. These are precisely the types of discourses that teachers did not want articulated in schools. Faced with a group of students who most obviously experience the structural legacies of apartheid, Mr. Lane did not wish to "ingrain" ideas that would prevent them from embracing ideologies of individualism and hard work. For these students, who articulated more critical views, it is possible that the simulation would have made the past more alive, rather than distant.

SIMULATIONS

Mr. Lane may have had an additional concern: that 9M would interpret his role in the simulation as indicating that he personally held racist views. Mr. Lane was very aware of his relationship with 9M and proudly described his efforts to form a strong bond with the students in his class. Here is a portion of our exchange when I asked how students ended up in 9M:

> MR. LANE: . . . That was done because those kids were in six of seven separate classes last year. . . . So they were put in the class to try and keep them away from the others and when they got there and they saw who [else] was in the class, they imploded. That relationship that I have with them now, I've only had it [since] about four or five weeks . . . [prior to the end of] the last term. I was always fighting with them. . . . All of a sudden, I was able to turn the ringleaders.
>
> CHANA: What do you think helped you get a good relationship with them?
>
> MR. LANE: I think one of my strengths in real life is that I'm very, very hard initially and I slowly turn it. . . . And it's about figuring them out and realizing who they are [and letting them know that] they're not these useless things. . . . I said, "You believe you're stupid but you're not." . . . Hopefully it's a good thing and I hope [that because] it's a white guy doing it—by pure accident or luck or coincidence or whatever you want to call it, it's a white guy telling them [this] and maybe they can see there's a difference. Because there's women here—a couple of white women, the things they say to them, not

racist, but the things they [say] to them, you don't talk to people like that. I'm straight with them; I tell them, "You piece of shit or whatever," but you don't attack them at their core.

The contrast Mr. Lane drew between himself and other white teachers, who he said were "not racist" but belittled students, became clearer one day when I was observing 9M. Ms. Prescott, Mr. Pretorius, and a white male teacher I didn't know marched into Mr. Lane's classroom and together began to pat down the students and search through their backpacks. A teacher had reported her cellphone stolen and suggested that a student in 9M took it. Mr. Lane stood to the side as Ms. Prescott patted down the girls and the other two teachers patted down the boys. The students protested that none of them could have taken the phone because, at the beginning of the previous lesson, the teacher had walked into the classroom and said, "I'm useless! I forgot my phone in the other class!" They repeatedly insisted that they were receiving this treatment "just 'cause we're 9M." At the end of the period, with the cellphone still missing and the teachers gone, Mr. Lane and I walked out of the classroom together. He turned to me and said, "A whole year's work, gone, just like that."

I am not sure that Mr. Lane was correct in his assessment. From what I saw, students continued to have friendly interactions with him, and there was no dramatic change that I could discern. Nonetheless, the incident highlighted the tenuous relationship between students in 9M and white teachers in the school. Given this context, it may not be so surprising that

SIMULATIONS

Mr. Lane would think twice before taking on the role of the apartheid state in a simulation. Although I do not have access to the counterfactual scenario (what would have happened had Mr. Lane instituted the simulation), these data suggest that simulations may not function to distance the past if students have not already internalized the idea that the past has very little bearing on their lives.

REACTIONS FROM ROXBRIDGE HIGH

Over at Roxbridge High, I was curious whether the teachers had opinions about their colleagues' simulation exercises. Ms. Roux, a white Roxbridge teacher, lit up as I described the apartheid role-playing. "I think it's quite a nice activity," she said. "It's something completely different. Sure. Okay. No, that's quite a good idea." She added that it might depend on how mature the students in the class were, but she concluded, "That's a really good idea. I must remember it."

Ms. Viljoen (white), the head of the history department, responded similarly. When I asked whether she would ever consider instituting such an activity at Roxbridge, she said she would "leave it up to the teachers." To her, it seemed likely to be "a bigger lesson to learn for kids in [Roxbridge] Hoër," an Afrikaans-medium school where students tended to be white and middle class, than at Roxbridge High, where "kids . . . already have certain divisive factors. You have kids who live in squatter camps and are heads of their household at fifteen, and you have kids who come from families where they go overseas twice a year." She continued: "It's not that other schools don't have that, but English[-medium] schools definitely have it more than a homogenic [*sic*] school [like Roxbridge Hoër], that difference."[15] She concluded that she was not sure she would "have the heart" to do the simulation for a whole term and that she worried it might cause "meanness" on the playground. It seemed to me that Ms. Viljoen was suggesting, not that students would learn nothing from the simulation, but that it might exacerbate existing tensions—perhaps by foregrounding contemporary racial divisions rather than reinforcing the irrelevance of the past.

Ms. Devin (white) was also intrigued by the idea of a simulation, but she suggested that, rather than using race, she would consider segregating by something arbitrary, like shoe size.[16] Even so, she worried that "it might still be too sensitive for some kids whose parents were affected" by apartheid. She imagined that she would want to get permission from parents before doing a simulation in her classroom—even though she didn't think the school would require it. This response hinted that Glenville was not an outlier in granting teachers a lot of autonomy in designing and implementing classroom exercises.

Ms. Lesley was the only Roxbridge teacher who responded skeptically when I described the Glenville role-playing. At first, she was ambivalent, telling me she liked the idea, which reminded her of the Apartheid Museum, where visitors are randomly assigned to enter through separate doors for "whites" and "nonwhites."[17] But Ms. Lesley hesitated about whether she'd want to apply such rules to kids, concluding that it would be okay if students were allowed to choose their own race. Still, like Ms. Devin, she thought it would require debriefing because she would not want students and their parents to complain that she was being racist. "I just think you've got to be very careful in terms of parents, you know, how it goes back to a parent because [students] might say, 'The teacher was racist to me today' and they might not explain the whole exercise."

I asked Ms. Lesley if she thought a simulation would cause racial issues at school. Ms. Lesley did not directly answer my question, instead doubling back on her earlier support for the idea: "I don't know what the point would be of it [the simulation]," she said, "well, besides empathy . . . I'd be careful how I did that, if I did it." As I moved to my next question, she interrupted me, wanting to return to the question of the simulation. It seemed she had, in the course of talking it through, come to a firm position that role-playing had no place in high school history education:

> Any kind of role-playing in history I don't agree with because . . . how could they possibly have that knowledge? How could they possibly ever understand? . . . Yes, it gives them a chance to act and be creative and think out of the box but to put yourself in somebody else's shoes is a skill that most adults don't even understand. It's really a difficult thing. And then to put on thousands of years of discrimination and—it kind of undermines it and then you've got the kids laughing at it and I kind of—I don't like [it]. It's something in me that I just feel, "Oh, I'm not comfortable with that."

In rethinking the idea of role-playing, Ms. Lesley concluded not that it would heighten racial tensions—as she had indicated initially—but that it would trivialize the past. Perhaps both scenarios are true. In some contexts, role-playing may create racialized conflict among students or between teachers and students. In other contexts, simulations may present the past as something so distant and incomprehensible that the exercise becomes a game in which the past has no bearing on students' lived realities.

In general, teachers at Roxbridge High seemed hesitant about the idea of a simulation and gave reasons that fit with Mr. Lane's over at Glenville. African students at Roxbridge who came from low-income families were not segregated into "Zulu classes," and the school enrolled many more white students than did Glenville. In such a context, simulations might be riskier in terms of their ability to impinge on the present by highlighting continued structures of inequality. Such discussions of historical continuities contain within them the potential for student conflict at the intersection of race and class. Teachers, as we have seen throughout this book, tried to avoid such conflict in their schools and classrooms. So, while the practices of the two schools differed, both seemed to be driven by a similar underlying ideology of distancing the past from the present.

MISSED OPPORTUNITIES: THE SOCIAL CONSTRUCTION—AND REAL EFFECTS—OF RACE

At both Glenville and Roxbridge, teachers missed the opportunity to open a conversation about the nature of race and its effects on South African society, both past and present. At Glenville, the simulation resulted in students and teachers regulating racial boundaries by categorizing each other. In allowing this to happen unexamined, teachers treated racial categories as fixed and objective. At the same time, they sidelined discussions of the real effects of race on people's daily lives.

In Ms. Mokoena's classroom, for instance, an Indian student wondered what would happen during apartheid "if a black person gave birth to an albino child." Ms. Mokoena answered, "Young man, if it's an albino, an albino has spongy hair. . . . And our noses are African noses." Pointing to a phenotypical understanding of race, she did not open a conversation about the social constructions of these categories. She reminded the class of a previous lesson in which she had discussed the "pencil test"—one of the ways the apartheid state's racial categorizers (including the notorious Racial Classification Board) used to discern an individual's race.[18]

Many of the teachers spoke about the pencil test, in which officials checked to see whether a pencil inserted in a person's hair stayed in place (indicating that the person was African or possibly Coloured) or fell out (indicating that the person was white, Indian, or possibly Coloured), with some demonstrating it on themselves and others using student volunteers. Ms. Prescott simply walked up to a biracial student and put a pencil in the young woman's afro. Tucking the pencil into her own hair, Ms. Ndlovu explained: "You see, it doesn't fall. I am African. So, if it fell, it showed you were white or Coloured or Indian. It was [also] the color of your skin that they used. So [Amira] could have been mistaken for a white because she is so light-skinned. And then there were Coloureds who are so dark they could be classified as black [African]."

SIMULATIONS

Using their students and themselves—as racialized subjects—to teach about apartheid, teachers reinforced commonsense notions of race based on physical difference (such as hair texture and skin tone). At the same time, they presented the tests used by apartheid's racial classifiers as silly. Students laughed as teachers talked about hair and the varied ways such tests "got things wrong."[19] Paradoxically, they relied on racial assumptions as a backdrop against which to characterize the apartheid state's system of racial classification as ridiculous.

Even as they naturalized race through their historical role-playing, students and teachers suggested time and again that race no longer matters. In Ms. Ndlovu's classroom, students asked why they were still asked to indicate their race on official forms for things like school enrollment and identity document applications. Saying she wasn't sure, Ms. Ndlovu turned to me.

These were the types of moments I disliked most during my fieldwork. My approach to classroom observations was to be as nonintrusive as possible. When teachers asked me direct questions, I had to make on-the-spot decisions, usually sidestepping with comments like "I'm interested in hearing what you think." At that moment and in that classroom, however, I decided to offer my thoughts. I said that I thought the government wanted schools, for example, to ask students about their race so that it could see if things had changed in the new South Africa—to make sure that schools that were "whites only" during apartheid had now integrated and so on. I said that the government couldn't know if things had changed if it didn't keep this kind of information. My intervention seemed to resonate for an African student, who affirmed me and said that recordkeeping was intended "to fix the past." But other students jumped in, retorting that "but now it is all equal" and that "it is going back to apartheid."

The simulations seemed to reaffirm the dual notion that race was real but that it was also inconsequential. Building on shared commonsense notions of race, teachers and students categorized themselves and one another. However, armed with the idea that racial stratification is a thing of the past, they resisted racial counting and categorizing when done by the state for redress purposes.

■ ■ ■

Historical simulations at Glenville High reinforced ideas of distance between past and present by suggesting that students had no contemporary access to the realities of racial stratification and discrimination. At the same time, data from Mr. Lane's classroom and from Roxbridge High suggest that, in instances where students have not internalized the ideology of difference between "then" and "now," simulations can threaten to undermine lessons about the irrelevance of the past.

Overall, this chapter highlights how educators missed an opportunity to discuss the complex ways in which race, as a social construct, had—and continues to have—real material and symbolic effects on people's lives. In the next chapter, I turn to how this pedagogy of historical irrelevance affected students' ability to understand current policies aimed at redressing past injustices.

Chapter Five

CONSEQUENCES

HOW DID high school students—all, in South African parlance, "born frees" who never lived under apartheid—talk about the effects of that violent era of state-mandated racial segregation? Did their narratives differ before and after they encountered official curricula focused on apartheid in their history classes? The answers to these questions are not straightforward. Though students were more likely to link apartheid to contemporary social issues *after* taking the history module, *how* they linked past to present did not change. In both sets of interviews, students largely focused on the individual-level effects of apartheid while resisting structural arguments that highlighted the endurance of racialized inequality into the democratic era.

CONTEMPORARY SOCIAL PROBLEMS

Twenty-four percent of students in the pre-sample and 40 percent of students in the post-sample referenced apartheid as a

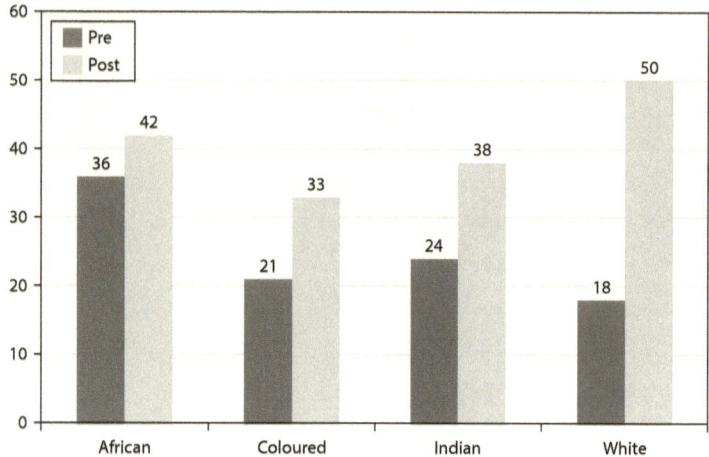

FIGURE 5.1 Percentage of students linking apartheid to current social problems, by race and sample ($N = 155$).

factor that explained a variety of contemporary social issues.[1] These included high levels of poverty, unemployment, and crime and low levels of educational attainment among sectors of the population. Figure 5.1 presents the breakdown of such responses by sample and race.

Students raised these issues at various points in our conversations. As part of the interview, I asked them to tell me about anything that made them feel particularly proud to be South African and anything that made them not so proud. The social problems that came up among their lists of "not so proud" aspects of their country gave me a moment to probe, asking the students to tell me, in their own words, *why* they thought South Africa had high crime, poverty, and unemployment rates or what could explain the fact that so many people didn't have a good education.

Their answers often linked these issues together, so that a student might begin by saying that they were not so proud of the country's high crime rates and then, asked to elaborate, tell me that crime is committed by people who don't have jobs and some individuals don't have jobs because they do not have an adequate education. At some point in the causal chain, fifty-one students attributed these issues, at least in part, to apartheid. An exchange with Tamryn, a Coloured student in the post-sample at Glenville, is illustrative:

> CHANA: And is there anything that you're not so proud of [in the country]?
> TAMRYN: The crime rates. The crime rates are very high in South Africa. . . .
> CHANA: And why do you think they are so high?
> TAMRYN: I think because lots of people aren't educated. . . .
> CHANA: And why do you think that so many people don't have an education?
> TAMRYN: I'd say because of the past, because apartheid deprived them and things, so it's not just going to take maybe ten or sixteen years for the effects of apartheid to just vanish and things. It takes a longer amount of time. So hopefully, over the next fifty years or whatever, it will be phased out and everything.

Students also spoke about contemporary social problems when, later in the interview, I asked more directly whether they thought apartheid still affected South Africa, as well as when, in the post-sample interviews, I asked whether learning about apartheid in school helped them understand present-day South Africa better. For example, Abigail, a white student in the post-sample at Roxbridge, gave a similar answer to Tamryn but introduced the notion of the intergenerational transmission of poverty:

> CHANA: And do you think that apartheid still affects the lives of South Africans today in any way?
> ABIGAIL: Yes, because people that were uneducated then have passed it on, and now they can't afford for their future generations to go to school, and they remain uneducated and poor.

Students in the post-sample, across all races, were more likely to make sense of current social problems by drawing on apartheid as a contributing factor. This was especially true for white students. Regardless of race, however, the ways that students deployed the past did not change. Whether focused on the individuals who lived during apartheid or on subsequent generations, students focused on the effects of *disadvantage*. Their explanations centered *poverty*, not *inequality*, and they often intimated that the social issues would naturally disappear over time. Some offered up job creation programs as a solution, but still others seemed resigned to the status quo, unable to think of any possible solutions. What none of the students did was argue in favor of structural interventions, such as affirmative action policies or wealth taxes.

CONSEQUENCES

Only Ntombi, an African student in one of Ms. Ndlovu's "Zulu classes" at Glenville, offered a more structural explanation, putting *disadvantage* in the context of *advantage*. She answered affirmatively when I asked her whether apartheid affects the lives of South Africans today, explaining:

> Because in some sense, black people are somehow still seen as a bit inferior to white people—because, as you can see, white people and other races are owning big houses and everything. If things were like equal, I think we will all live in big houses or be having our own businesses. But, right now, black people work for white people in everything, like domestic workers and everything, like black people clean the streets. So, I don't think it's that fair.

Ntombi's words illustrate the potential for students to develop other types of understandings of the legacies of apartheid—ones that focus less on the individual-level effects of *disadvantage* and more on the structural and relational effects of *inequality*. History lessons did not encourage these types of arguments; instead, as I have shown, they focused on listing the laws that disadvantaged blacks and the dates of their implementation. The post-sample students' greater knowledge of apartheid's laws in general may explain the increase in the number of students linking apartheid to current social problems. However, the fact that these lessons did not explore issues of white privilege alongside those related to black disadvantage left students without an understanding of apartheid as a system of legislated inequality—the effects of which continue into the present.

INTERPERSONAL RACISM

When students spoke about white South Africans, they spoke about individual-level prejudice, suggesting that this prejudice largely dissipated after the end of apartheid. A few intimated that whites' racist attitudes were *sometimes* intergenerationally transmitted, but generally they understood racism as an individual-level dislike of other races, a relic that lived, in the present, primarily in the minds of old people.

Take, for example, Abigail, a white student in the post-sample at Glenville who had told me about the intergenerational transmission of social problems created by apartheid. When it came to talking about white racism, however, she offered a much narrower view, focusing on older South Africans—like her parents and grandparents—who lived through apartheid, but disavowing the persistence of racism among young people like herself. In our interview, Abigail told me that her parents and grandparents wouldn't want her to date someone who wasn't white. When I asked why she thought that was the case, she explained that they had learned to be racist during apartheid. But she—a younger person in a racially diverse school—has learned other lessons:

> ABIGAIL: Well, I think my parents and grandparents—I think what they learnt was that black people were not good and that you were not to associate yourself with them. Whereas me, I've never learnt that. I've just seen them as [the same as] anyone [else], just the same as me. So I've learnt that they're friends, they're anything you want them to be. So I think that's it.

CONSEQUENCES

CHANA: But if your parents learnt those lessons, how come you're not learning that from them at home?
ABIGAIL: I think you learn most of your things at school.

Other students hinted that racist attitudes *could* be intergenerationally transmitted. But, like Abigail, they focused on racism as individual-level feelings of dislike rather than unequal racialized structures. For example, Rishi, an Indian student in the pre-sample at Glenville, commented that "a lot of fathers passed it [racism] down to their kids" and that, "if their father says, 'Don't be friends with that [race],' then they'll also think, like, 'Oh, they're bad.'"

Except for the slight decrease among white respondents, I heard these explanations more in the post-sample than in the pre-sample (see figure 5.2). Still, African students were least likely to talk about continued white racism in both waves of interviews. Their hesitance may involve interviewer effects, in which African students may have been reluctant to disclose their views on white racism to me—a white interviewer. If that were the case, however, it is unclear why this effect would have held among Africans but not Coloureds or Indians. Interviewer effects that are traceable to race in the South African context are ripe for systematic sociological attention.

For our purposes and with current knowledge, there are several ways to make sense of this finding. First, African students told me many stories that they did not see as demonstrating racism, though I did. If they felt uncomfortable disclosing experiences of racism to a white interviewer, I would have expected them to withhold these stories. Instead, they told them and

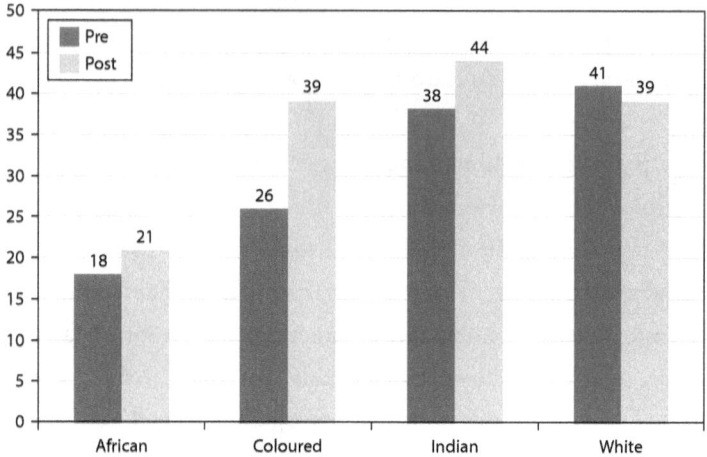

FIGURE 5.2 Percentage of students linking apartheid to whites' interpersonal racism, by race and sample ($N = 155$).

then did a lot of work to explain to me why apparently racist incidents were not, in fact, racially motivated. Second—as I have shown in previous chapters—teachers carefully framed the history of apartheid in a way that limited students' ability to make connections between the racialized past and the racialized present and that delegitimized claims about contemporary racism. That African students were hesitant to code the incidents they shared as "racist" (yet shared in the context of interviews one could easily say were *about racism*) may indicate that they—more than other students—are penalized for sharing such interpretations and have learned not to do so in the school context (and possibly beyond).[2]

CONSEQUENCES

Those African students who *did* talk about the effects of apartheid on whites' views of blacks tended to do so in the same ways as white, Indian, and Coloured students—conceptualizing racism as a remnant of the past, carried by older people who lived through apartheid. Hope, an African student in the post-sample at Glenville, told me, "The young white people understand how we [Africans] feel, but the older people, they still don't like us.... *Ja* [yes], it's the older generation who has been through the apartheid system." I reiterated to confirm, "And what about people your age?" Hope again said definitively, "Our age? No."

While black African students were reticent to talk about the persistence of white racism, they were surprisingly likely to tell me that black South Africans today *illegitimately* believe they are owed something because of apartheid.

REVENGE, GRUDGES, AND EXCUSES

Over a third of the students I interviewed took up the argument that apartheid affects contemporary South Africa because black South Africans simply refuse to let it go. Students commented that black South Africans hold on to apartheid, use it as an excuse, and seek revenge against whites as a collective.

This discourse is very similar to David Sears's identification of "symbolic racism" in the post–civil rights United States. According to Sears, "old fashioned racism" (beliefs in the innate inferiority of blacks and support of formal and de jure discrimination) may be disappearing in a civil liberties United States, but racism has not disappeared. Instead, racism has taken on a new form, symbolic racism, which combines anti-black affect with traditional American values (for example, individualism and a Protestant work ethic). Symbolic racist attitudes are articulated in a variety of ways, including "resentment toward special favors for blacks, such as in 'reverse discrimination,' racial quotas in jobs or education, excessive access to welfare, special treatment by government, or unfair and excessive gain by blacks . . . the belief that discrimination in areas such as jobs or housing is a thing of the past because blacks now have the freedom to compete in the marketplace and to enjoy things they can afford."[3]

The concept of symbolic racism is similar to Lawrence Bobo and colleagues' theory of laissez-faire racism, in which black-white gaps in achievement are attributed to blacks' cultural deficiencies in a supposedly fair market. According to Bobo, Kluegel, and Smith, racism emanates not from whites' affective dislike of blacks or from their individual self-interest, but from their collective sense of group position.[4] While these authors debate the origins, nature, and appropriate measurement of less overt types of racism, they are united by their emphasis on how new forms of prejudice combine "racial and supposedly non-racial attitudes . . . [and] block public policies that could reduce racial inequality."[5] In other words, racism yields racist outcomes, whatever its form.

Take for instance, Madison, a white student in the post-sample at Glenville, who in her interview with me recalled a time when two black students told her not to think she was better than them because she was white: "I just told them,

'I can't believe you guys are saying this. Apartheid's over. It's done and over with. Are you guys racist now?' I said, 'It's over now . . . by the time you were born, apartheid was over.'"

Reflecting on this example, I asked Madison whether she thought people her age were still holding on to apartheid. "Some are," she answered, "like they [black South Africans] have grudges against us [white South Africans] because of their families that are struggling now at the moment and everything—so they take it out on us." That white students would make these arguments was not entirely surprising. But, as seen in figure 5.3, this idea was expressed by students across race, with African students in the post-sample employing this explanation most frequently.

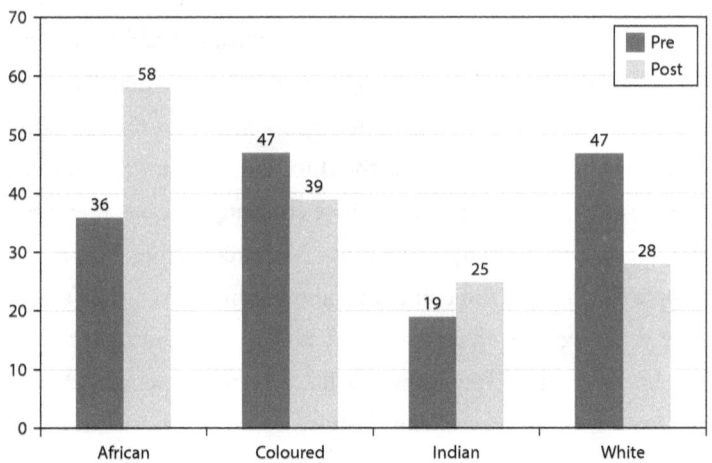

FIGURE 5.3 Percentage of students linking apartheid to blacks' feelings of revenge, grudges, and excuses, by race and sample ($N = 155$).

When I asked Mpho, an African student in the post-sample at Glenville, about contemporary discrimination in South Africa, he immediately thought of anti-white sentiments. "I think some black people still hold a grudge against some white people," he responded quickly. Naledi, an African student in the post-sample at Roxbridge, gave a similar response, using Julius Malema—the head of the Economic Freedom Fighters (discussed in chapters 1, 4 and the conclusion)—as an example of how black South Africans discriminate against whites: "He has so much hate speech against the white race. . . . I mean, we had apartheid about—how many years ago—seventeen years ago? And he is still going to bring back the past, and I mean, it's just useless. If you're going to like start bringing up things of the past and start being all racist, it's not going to solve anything. . . . I don't like the way he has so much hate speech against white people, so much racism, so much discrimination."

Thandiwe, an African student at Roxbridge, said much the same, insisting that blacks illegitimately blame whites in contemporary South Africa for their problems. She thought this disingenuity could cause apartheid to "come back." I asked her to tell me a bit more, and Thandiwe continued: "Like, if you see the news, so many people like Julius Malema . . . there's so many people that say hurtful comments about whites. And they're not over it; you can see that they're not over it, and they want to get, you know, in rule. They want to kill . . . the white people. One of my friends is white, and she's very scared that apartheid might come back to them. It's not their [whites'] fault, you know."

The idea that apartheid might return—but that, in this version, whites would be discriminated against—was repeated throughout my interviews. It was especially present during discussions of affirmative action–style Black Economic Empowerment (BEE) policies. Monique, a Coloured student in the Glenville pre-sample, described these policies as a form of "vice versa" apartheid and an example of how the current government was taking "revenge" against white people:

> Almost like in apartheid again because, with this whole BEE thing, it's like excluding white people. Now it's just vice versa. It's almost like [President] Zuma wants to take revenge on those white people, you see.[6] I think that's like ridiculous. *Ja*, it's really ridiculous. . . . I want to say that, like with this whole apartheid story, it's been like a huge lesson for South Africa. But it's almost like some people aren't really soaking it into their brains, because like with this whole BEE thing, you know, [President] Zuma is just doing it again, and it's not right.

Like Monique, Riley, a white student in the post-sample at Roxbridge, listed revenge among the drivers of blacks' receiving opportunities in the new South Africa: "I'm not meaning to be a racist or anything, but the blacks are, they're getting most of the opportunities. And I think that how it should work is everyone—it's according to your ability not to your race or anything. . . . I think some of them want revenge [for] apartheid."

Several African students told me about family members who held the kinds of views the students criticized. Early in my interviews, I asked students a series of questions meant to tap different aspects of their identities. When I asked Judith, an African student in the post-sample at Glenville, to tell me what being black meant to her, she expressed a type of color-blindness, telling me that "being black is like being any other race—you must work hard, it doesn't matter what color you are." She elaborated that what she *didn't* like was the idea that "when you're black, you feel like you deserve something because so-and-so happened a hundred years ago." Later, Judith presented her sister as a foil to her own beliefs, explaining that her sister *illegitimately* believes that whites "owe her or her family or all of us something":

> CHANA: Do you ever talk about apartheid at home?
> JUDITH: *Ja*, especially with my sister because she's also got that mentality that white people owe her or her family or all of us something. *Ja*, so like we're always debating on that.
> CHANA: Okay. So, could you walk me through a debate that you might have?
> JUDITH: Like she'd say—you know she's a domestic worker—then she'd say: "Someone else or like a white person should be doing this for me. I shouldn't be doing this because we've been doing this for the past—since those years, and we still do it. The country's not going forward." So I'd tell her: "Apartheid ended in 1994," and that's when she had a baby. Instead of giving birth—like it gets crucial—[I say:] "Instead of having a baby, you should've done something." Like we just fight about that all the time.
> CHANA: So why do you think that you have such a different perspective to her?

JUDITH: I think it's because I grew [up] around white people, and I know them better. Not all of them are racist. I don't feel from what I've learnt and seen about white people; I haven't seen any white person that owes me something. It's about getting what you want, not someone giving you what you think you deserve.

In this interchange, Judith told me how her sister, a domestic worker, identified structural legacies of apartheid and said that she had not seen transformation in race relations in her day-to-day life in a democratic South Africa. In saying that her sister believes white people "owe her something," Judith points to her sister's belief in the relational nature of inequality. In a sense, the sister's perspective highlights that whites benefited from the oppression of blacks and that real redress has not occurred. But Judith suggested to me that her sister was wrong—she was in her current situation because of her own decisions. While her sister focuses on structural racism, Judith reveals her own focus on interpersonal racism. Still later in our interview, when I asked Judith whether she thought there was discrimination in contemporary South Africa, she responded in the discourse of individualism:

CHANA: What about in the broader South African society? Do you think there's still discrimination and racism?
JUDITH: I think the people who are angry and racist are the people who don't have things to fall back on, like people with no money, no jobs, no cars. They feel, "I don't have so-so-so because I'm black." They don't think: "I don't have this, this [and] this because I didn't work for it."

CONSEQUENCES

Like their peers who focused on the individual-level effects of apartheid (and limited them to those who lived through it), students who spoke about revenge, grudges, and excuses failed to understand the ongoing structural effects of apartheid. Indeed, these students suggested that focusing on the past was irrational and unjustified.

These ideas, shared with me by students, were affirmed by teachers in the classrooms I observed. Recall Mr. Lane's 9M black African "Zulu class" from the previous chapter. In the middle of class one day, this educator simply asked his students how learning about apartheid made them feel. Despite the open-ended question, it soon became clear that Mr. Lane was setting himself up to impart a clear message to his students that they should let go of the past, reject structural explanations for continued inequality, and focus on individuals rather than groups when thinking through racism.

Students responded to Mr. Lane's question in ways that resonated with the historical distancing that characterized formal teaching at the school. "When we're at home," said one student, "you get different people's experience, but when you get [to] school, you learn about it not [from] someone else's emotions." Another responded: "One thing that makes me so angry is that black people fought for a difference. Now they have the opportunity, and they're messing it up." Cheering these students' responses, Mr. Lane responded: "It's nice to hear some intelligence coming out of your mouth." He summarized the conversation with the following assessment: "There seems to be . . . frustration. You are angry because your people have made this country worse."

CONSEQUENCES

Just then, a student interjected tentatively, "The ANC says we must not forget about the past." At that point I thought the conversation might shift to a critique of the discourse of historical irrelevance. But another student jumped in, dismissing this critique as irrational. She said: "The ANC are saying don't forget about our racial past 'cause it [freedom] might be snatched away. Why do they do that? They are putting fear. But they are not so bright, 'cause how could a small minority take over the vote?" Here, Mr. Lane again lent his support: "If you're frustrated, I'm glad, 'cause the majority are not."

With that, the teacher pointed to a student who had been quiet throughout the conversation. "I think it's your turn to speak," Mr. Lane commented. The African student offered, "The people I'm surrounded by feel like, 'Okay guys, now you deserve this.' But if I didn't learn at this school, what would my state of mind be when I saw white people? I would be angry. For what reason, I don't know." Mr. Lane seemed to think this was a good response and added that the ANC, like the National Party during apartheid, used political fearmongering: "The National Party built the country on fear. Now the ANC is building it on fear too. It's because they don't have a vision [that] they are appealing to the most basic thing you have in your body: Fear."

When a student *did* introduce a critical perspective, she did so by pointing out what seemed to her a rather obvious, present-day racial inequality: "You know there will always be a thing of race. You see schools that are white, and they look better, and you see schools in Soweto, and they look [worse]." Mr. Lane did not engage the student's point by attending to resource allocation or the ongoing effects of apartheid's racial geography. Instead, he homed in on the desegregated nature of *this* school. "How many whites are here?" he asked. "There are like twelve," chimed in another student. But the first student pressed on, responding, "Yes, but it being in [Glenville makes] it . . . glamorous. But when you go to Soweto, it doesn't look pretty. It will always be a question of race." Mr. Lane again sidestepped the structural issues. "Why are Soweto schools so bad?" he asked, before answering his own question: "'Cause they want it for free."

Recalling a school he had attended in the past, another student seemed to shift the conversation: "In primary school, I had an Indian teacher [and] she still hates blacks even now. 'Cause she said, 'you get black billionaires, but they still flash around the past.'" In that moment, I wondered if this student was subtly suggesting that—like the primary school teacher who didn't want blacks to talk about the past—Mr. Lane was also being racist. Immediately, Mr. Lane shot back, "Why do I dislike you and not her—and you're both black?" Gesturing at his students and declaring he disliked one and not another, Mr. Lane encapsulated the messages he'd transmitted throughout the apartheid section: the past is past, racism no longer structures South African society, and it is up to the individual to make the most of the equal opportunities available in the present. Closing the conversation and moving back to his formal lesson plan, Mr. Lane reiterated: "It's not because I'm racist. You can't think like that anymore. You guys are the next generation."

■ ■ ■

CONSEQUENCES

Teachers in the South African schools I observed taught about apartheid in ways that distanced it from students' lived realities and obscured continued, structural, racialized inequality. These lessons reinforced and amplified ideas that were circulating among the students before they took the history module in school by lending them an official, educator's imprimatur. With rare exceptions, students sidestepped any ongoing structural effects attributable to apartheid. Instead, they perceived racism as interpersonal and out-of-date—something that probably affected those individuals who lived through the apartheid era but was irrelevant in the present and sure to die out quickly. They critiqued black South Africans who refuse to let apartheid go, arguing that they *irrationally* believe they are owed something in the new dispensation. Black African students were especially likely to express these views *after* they learned about apartheid in school, suggesting these lessons taught them to actively distance themselves from discourses advancing racial redress in the context of their formerly white, now desegregated, Rainbow Nation schools.

CONCLUSION

> *If I look at my kids interacting with each other, sometimes I wish I had it when I was . . . in school. Sometimes I actually envy them because they get to learn so many [more] different cultures than I had the opportunity to.*
>
> Ms. Roux, white, Roxbridge

ROXBRIDGE AND Glenville High are, in many ways, icons of transformation. Once reserved for whites only, both are now racially and socioeconomically diverse. They remain top-performing schools, offering opportunities for upward mobility for those disadvantaged by apartheid crimes.

Like Ms. Roux, quoted above, other teachers in my study celebrated the diversity of their schools. Over at Glenville, Ms. Ndlovu taught her students about the Freedom Charter by projecting a picture of a multiracial group of Glenville learners on the screen in her classroom.[1] "The doors of learning shall be opened," she declared, quoting from the charter. She described the picture: "You can see there is diversity there. There are Coloureds and Indians and black [African] and white." Then she named some Grade 9 students to drive home her point: Nathan Meyer was white, the Abrahams sisters were Coloured, Bongani was black African. "And our Indian boys," she added,

CONCLUSION

nodding at a group of Indian students in her classroom. Glenville, she was explaining, was itself the realization of the dreams and hopes of the anti-apartheid movement. The doors of learning had opened, and here they were, sitting in their desegregated classrooms. Ms. Ndlovu concluded, "So multiracial! That is [Glenville]."

Teachers were not the only ones who felt proud of the diversity of their schools. When I asked what being South African meant to them, 63.3 percent of the learners said it meant living in a diverse society and interacting across racial lines. Many linked their descriptions of diversity as a national characteristic with their experiences at school. For example, Madison, a white Glenville student, told me that being South African makes her "proud because we've been through so much with everything, and today we can still sit together in a class, all mixed races."

Asked the same question, Njabulo, an African Roxbridge student, pointed out that the country now recognized eleven official languages. I asked him to elaborate—how would he describe South Africa to someone who had never been there? "I think I'd say first . . . that we don't look at race that much," he said. "Race is out of the picture now."

Again, I probed, asking him to elaborate. Njabulo turned to using the school itself as an example: "For instance, if you look out the window it's not just black people playing netball or white people, it's every race because we see everybody as one big family now."[2] He then recalled something his teacher the previous year used to say: "The class is not separated as black, white, Coloured, Indian. We're just all together. Because, once you walk through the door, it's no more 'I'm black,' 'I'm white,'

CONCLUSION

'I'm Coloured,' it's all about 'We're here together as a school, and we'll be one body.'"

Are we to conclude, then, that Glenville and Roxbridge High are success stories "in the battle for transformation"?[3] Do they represent the fulfilment of a multiracial Rainbow Nation, unbridled by the burdens of the past? My answer to these questions is, not quite. Throughout these pages, we have seen the costs of sustaining this image. The image is tenuous. It rests on a denial of the realities of enduring racism. And it is propped up by a particular telling of history—one that strives to leave the past in the past.

Recall Siyanda from chapter 1. Although Siyanda experienced everyday interpersonal and structural racism, she also wanted to "move away from the fact that there was apartheid." If her parents wanted her to have "a bright future," she told me, they would have to teach her that racial boundaries were a thing of the past. Her assessment seems to be correct—at least as far as her school context is concerned. For her ideas to continue to be validated by teachers in her formerly white, now Rainbow Nation school, Siyanda understood that she could not dwell on the past or on contemporary racial inequality.

These findings push us to think about inequality in schools beyond academic outcomes (things like the students' grades, graduation rates, and college admissions) and their relationship with occupational achievement (the jobs students eventually end up in).[4] Instead, they bring our attention to the *unequal experiences* that young people have within schools and classrooms. They also foreground the role of schooling in teaching broad *lessons about inequality*. The preceding pages show how

CONCLUSION

black students were silenced when they raised issues that connected past to present and insisted on the continued salience of racism in South Africa. Ironically, by validating the perspectives of dominant groups, teachers could present their schools as models of racial reconciliation and diversity.

Further, in muting discussions of apartheid's legacies, teachers taught lessons with broad political consequences for social inequality.[5] Children and adolescents, after all, are not just future workers. They are also future voters and decision-makers, and how they learn to understand social inequality in school will impact those roles. Glenville and Roxbridge presented themselves as models of transformation. But they did so by teaching lessons that hindered political action aimed at redressing racism's ongoing effects.

BEYOND GLENVILLE AND ROXBRIDGE

This book is not an exposé of two schools. It is a piece of sociological research that uses two schools as case studies to help us understand something about racism, collective memory, and education in post-apartheid South Africa.[6] It is standard ethical practice in social scientific research to ensure participants' privacy and minimize any potential harm that may come from participating in a study, and so I have anonymized the names of schools, teachers, and students. Yet, as I write, I realize that the anonymization also helps us resist the temptation to identify the problem exclusively with these two schools and their teachers. Such approaches individualize the systemic issues underscored by my research.

CONCLUSION

The teachers in my study did not pull things out of thin air. They worked within a centralized national curriculum that demarcated where—and in relation to what—apartheid should be taught. Before they even stepped into the classroom, teachers were operating within a system that juxtaposed apartheid with historical events from other times and in other parts of the world. This curricular structure contributed to the compartmentalizing of apartheid as an event that came and went, rather than as part of a structural story of racism and dispossession that stretches back to colonialism and continues through contemporary racialized inequality.

Once they did step into the classroom, teachers had a lot of autonomy in deciding how to flesh out content headings provided by the centralized national curriculum. Here, too, they operated in a broader context, drawing on narratives that resonated with those institutionalized during the country's transition to democracy. Glenville and Roxbridge teachers did not know one another, let alone work together to construct their lesson plans. Yet they taught about apartheid in surprisingly *similar* ways, despite the large degree of autonomy they had in designing their lessons. They did so, it seems, because they were drawing on wider narratives and resources that make up the cultural "tool-kit" of post-apartheid South Africa.[7]

When I write that the teachers actively drew on wider narratives, I do not mean to imply that there were no alternatives. Even at the time of my fieldwork, other ideas were circulating in South African public discourse. For instance, shortly after I left the field, South Africa saw the consolidation of a new political party—the Economic Freedom Fighters (EFF). Its

CONCLUSION

leader was Julius Malema—the former ANC Youth League leader who was presented in classrooms as the embodiment of irrational desires for revenge. Teachers positioned Malema's ideas as ridiculous. But Malema and his party have garnered much support. In the first elections they contested in 2014, they won several municipalities and approximately six percent of the popular vote, thus placing third overall. By 2019, in the second general elections they contested, they increased their share of the popular vote to ten percent. The EFF's campaign platforms include several forms of redress and reparations, such as land redistribution, the righting of apartheid's economic crimes, and the dismantling of "white monopoly capital."[8] Others have written (both favorably and critically) about the rhetorical strategies and political objectives of the EFF.[9] What is indisputable is that the EFF represents an insistence on the continued relevance of the past, actively critiquing agendas that seek to distance it.

The EFF is not the only group making connections between historical and contemporary injustices. Similar ideas have also come to the fore in the Rhodes Must Fall and Fees Must Fall movements. In 2015, at the University of Cape Town (UCT)—an elite, formerly white, university—a black African student, Chumani Maxwele, threw a bucket of excrement onto a statue of colonialist Cecil John Rhodes that stood centrally on campus. Soon, demands that "Rhodes Must Fall" began to echo through—and beyond—the campus. Rhodes *did* fall—the statue was removed. But the movement continued, as students linked their struggle *against* colonial iconography with their struggle *for* decolonized free education.

CONCLUSION

It was not long before students at another elite, formerly white, university—the University of the Witwatersrand (Wits)—mobilized under the slogan "Fees Must Fall," calling for an end to the exclusionary costs of higher education in South Africa. Students at UCT joined in, as did those at other universities, including historically black universities. At one of the protests, a student held a placard that succinctly captured the sentiment that the past had not been dealt with. It said: "Our parents were sold a dream in 1994. We're just here for the refund."

On the face of it, it's surprising that these movements grew so powerfully in the racially diverse settings of UCT and Wits. Like Glenville and Roxbridge, these are educational spaces that facilitate upward mobility, where the historical conflation of race and class can be dismantled. The optics scream transformation. But scratch the surface, said the protestors, and it is clear that these remain white spaces under the material and figurative specter of white supremacy.[10]

When university students protested the Rhodes memorial, they made clear connections between the racist past and present. The protests were never just about demolishing a statue. They were about rejecting the idea that apartheid had been overcome. They were about saying that the past *does* matter; that it continues to structure *their* present; and that the architecture of colonialism and apartheid—not just its monuments and memorials, but its neighborhoods, schools, and universities, as well as its practices of inclusion and exclusion—needs to come down too.

These are just a couple of examples of how South Africans are making connections between past and present. In making these links, they are challenging and rejecting a narrative of rupture between past and present. But there *is* a clear narrative that they are arguing against. And this is the narrative I have documented in this book. To understand both color-blindness and its rejection, we must come to grips with the narratives that underpin it, including the central one that denies the relevance of the past for the present.

Students at Glenville and Roxbridge occasionally raised issues of structural inequality, linking past to present, and expressing a critical consciousness not taught in school. Teachers managed and contained these interventions, avoiding conversations of enduring racism and the conflict that such topics could spark. Although they drew on dominant narratives circulating in society, the teachers were not "cultural dopes,"[11] blindly reproducing these narratives. Instead, they actively distanced the past from present debates to sidestep difficult feelings and minimize conflict in their classrooms.

It should not be surprising that teachers wanted to avoid guilt, anger, and the conflict these emotions might ignite. Such conflict could have negative consequences for teachers themselves (think here about what it would mean for a teacher's reputation if their classroom was louder and more discordant than others). But it could also affect student learning and well-being. Teachers believed that students were better served by lessons that left the past in the past and foregrounded individual agency in the present. Many students expressed similar sentiments. To succeed in post-apartheid South Africa, they would need to work hard and not be drawn into historical disputes. But, as I have shown in the preceding pages, distancing the past is not a

CONCLUSION

neutral endeavour. It silences those who want to engage the past to understand their lived reality, and it socializes young people away from collective action.

South Africa is not the only country facing challenges around teaching its nation's history of racial oppression. As I write this conclusion, the spotlight is on history education in the United States. There, a backlash is taking place against the teaching of "critical race theory" in the school curriculum. It is doubtful that most high schools, let alone elementary schools, are teaching legal theory. (The term "critical race theory" refers to a framework developed by legal scholars to understand how racism has been—and continues to be—embedded in the law).[12] At its core, however, the rallying cry reflects a resistance to schools' engagement (however meager) with the country's racist past and present.

This backlash came as a response to the rise of public support for the racial reckoning demanded by the Black Lives Matter (BLM) movement.[13] An explicitly race-conscious social movement, BLM asserted that racism had not been dealt with—but it must be. Its rise in prominence was met with color-blind (but deeply racially coded) slogans like "All Lives Matter" and moves to control the narrative by recrafting history education. Right now, U.S. states are banning books and regulating school curricula. The attack on history education puts a spotlight on how threatening discussions of white privilege are to those who hold that privilege. It reminds us that history makes demands of the present and can be used to mobilize for justice. No wonder the fight *against* racial justice has turned not to history's lessons, but history lessons.

CONCLUSION

Erasure and denial are not the only ways to suppress demands made by the past.[14] Indeed, such overt strategies are often easy to identify and critique. But silencing can take other, more covert forms that exist alongside mnemonic talk, hiding in plain sight.[15] As this book has shown, apartheid is very much present in the South African school curriculum. In fact, there are currently moves to give it a more central role, making it a mandatory school subject beyond the ninth grade.[16] But it is taught in a way that neutralizes and pacifies, where connections to the present are muted and ignored.

As time passes, such pressing historical connections could find their way into history classrooms more frequently, amplifying discussions of how the past shapes the present. Such conversations could cause conflict in schools and beyond. But they might also open a space for political action aimed at remedying past injustices and the enduring inequalities that these injustices have wrought. *Distancing the Past* serves as a record of what happened as the first generation after apartheid sat in their desegregated history classrooms. History will teach us whether and how things changed.

ACKNOWLEDGMENTS

IN MANY ways, this book is a critique of pedagogical practices at Glenville and Roxbridge. I hope that I have shown that my critique is not of individual schools or teachers, but of broader discourses and currents that manifest in particular ways in the racially diverse schools that I studied. I would not have been able to write this book without the schools opening their doors to me. So, my thanks are fraught. I am grateful to the educators who believed enough in this project to welcome me into their schools and classrooms. They did so because they wanted to help make history teaching better. The critiques that I have offered come from the same intention. I thank these history educators for generously sharing their thoughts and experiences with me, and I hope that this book is read with the spirit of constructive critique and a shared view to making things better.

I am equally indebted to the learners who agreed to participate in this study. They sat with me after a long day at school and told me about much more than history. I thank them for their enthusiasm, depth, sense of humor, and generous willingness to talk about schoolwork after school hours.

I began this project as a graduate student at Harvard. There, I was supported by a team of incredible mentors. Mary Waters struck the perfect balance between guiding me along the way and letting me do my own thing. I thank her for her practical advice on how to tackle a big project (write in chunks), her amazing ability to get to the core of an argument, and her appreciation of the nuance of the story. Most importantly, I thank her for always seeing me as a whole person, with a life outside of academia—and for celebrating the nonacademic milestones as joyfully as she did the academic ones. Jocelyn Viterna was there every step of the way. I cannot imagine my graduate school years without her. She has provided me with more professional and intellectual advice than I could ever have hoped for. She is generous and kind and brilliant, and I am exceptionally grateful for all she has done to help me over the years. William Julius Wilson encouraged me to keep focused not only on the discipline-specific contributions of my study but also—and more importantly—on the social significance of my work. I thank him for asking—and encouraging me to try to answer—big questions. Bart Bonikowski's incisive feedback on early drafts completely reshaped how I was thinking about the project and helped me home in on the argument I was making. His input, encouragement, and support have been invaluable.

I am lucky to have found so many incredible friends in graduate school. I am even luckier that these friends also happen to be brilliant scholars. Brenna Powell, Graziella Moraes Silva,

ACKNOWLEDGMENTS

Lauren Rivera, and Simone Ispa-Landa are fantastic advice givers who provided me with very helpful feedback on different aspects of this manuscript. This book began to take shape during workdates with Cassi Pittman Claytor. I am grateful for her insightful feedback and supportive encouragement at crucial stages of my writing. Tracey Lloyd taught me about data management and so much more! She, Kim Pernell-Gallagher, and Eleni Arzoglou are my trouble-shooting team extraordinaire, talking me through all the conundrums along the way. Anmol Chaddha never tired of stories from the field. His reactions to those stories were—as his observations usually are—incredibly perceptive. Kevin Lewis is an incisive reader with a remarkable ability to pay attention to detail while keeping track of the big picture. I am immensely grateful for his brilliant feedback and advice. My work also benefited tremendously from conversations with Tamara Pavasović Trošt, Nicole Hirsch, Eva Rosen, Matt Kaliner, and Lauren Paremoer. I thank them for their friendship and collegiality. For feedback on early iterations of this work, I also thank members of Harvard's Weatherhead Center Graduate Student Associate lunch seminars, Culture and Social Analysis Workshop, and Sociology of Education Workshop.

Vered Vinitzky-Seroussi introduced me to the field of collective memory and inspired me to study it sociologically. I am enormously grateful for her ongoing mentorship. Thank you also to Jeffrey Olick, Joachim Savelsberg, Prudence Carter, Michèle Lamont, and David Cunningham, who have all provided me with excellent advice and feedback over the years. Thank you also to Kara Young and Jennifer Eaglin for their supportive feedback on chapter 1.

ACKNOWLEDGMENTS

Kammila Naidoo welcomed me to the University of Johannesburg (UJ) and gave me outstanding advice and support. For helpful comments and conversation, I also thank UJ colleagues Tapiwa Chagonda, Carin Runciman, and Marc Fletcher. I was fortunate to meet some incredible scholars of race, education, history, and memory in South Africa who generously engaged with my work. Thank you to Siobhan Glanvill, Rob Pattman, Deevia Bhana, Tamara Shefer, Kopano Ratele, Ronnelle Carollisen, Jill Bradbury, and Hugo Canham, as well as audiences at the Fourth Apartheid Archive Conference in Pretoria, the Narrative Enquiry for Social Transformation (NEST) Colloquium at Wits, the University of Johannesburg Wednesday Seminar, and the Colloquium on Young People Engaging in/ for Non-Violence and Equality at the Institute for Advanced Study at Stellenbosch University (STIAS).

At the London School of Economics and Political Science (LSE), Mike Savage has been generous with his time and helped me navigate life as an assistant professor. I am most grateful for his careful reading of my work. Aliya Hamid Rao, Rebecca Elliott, and Gözde Güran kept me on track in our writing accountability group, giving me trenchant feedback and sage counsel. I could not have asked for better colleagues. I also thank audiences at the LSE's III Migration, Ethnicity and Race seminar series as well as at the Department of Sociology Seminar.

Parts of this book draw on articles I published in the *American Journal of Sociology*, the *American Sociological Review*, and *Sociology of Education*. I thank the editors and anonymous reviewers of these journals for their comments and suggestions. I am also grateful to audiences at the American, British, and

ACKNOWLEDGMENTS

South African Sociological Association annual conferences, the Memory Studies Association annual conference, the Conflict and Identity Conference at Oxford, and the Figuring Memory Seminar at the American University, Paris—and in particular, to Sandrine Lefranc for her insightful discussant comments.

I gratefully acknowledge the generous support provided by the National Research Foundation, the National Science Foundation, the Harvard Academy for International and Area Studies, Harvard's Graduate School of Arts and Sciences (GSAS), and Harvard's Weatherhead Center for International Affairs.

Thank you to my editor at Columbia University Press, Eric Schwartz, for believing in this project and walking me through all the stages of publishing my first book. He made the process smoother than I could ever have imagined it to be. Thank you to wordsmith extraordinaire Letta Page for her thoughtful and careful edits to the draft manuscript and to Marisa Lastres, Susan Zorn, and Ben Kolstad for their copyedits to the final submission.

Finally, my thanks go to my family. I have no better friends than my sisters, Yehudit Orkin, Orya Shantall, and Sefi Avreky. I thank them for being there for me on all my journeys. Thank you to my parents, Alan and Rena Teeger for always supporting and believing in me unconditionally; and for teaching me to ask questions and to look beyond the surface of things. It is difficult for me to express the gratitude I feel for my partner, Dror Cohen. This project started before I met him. But it would have never been completed without him. He has supported, encouraged, and stood by me through it all. I am forever grateful. To our daughter, Ella Ray Cohen, thank you for being the best part of my day, every day.

METHODOLOGICAL APPENDIX

CASES

The schools chosen for this study are not meant to be representative of all South African schools. Rather than using the logic of statistical sampling—which, as Mario Luis Small has argued, is not the most fruitful way of conceptualizing this type of research—I sampled on theoretical grounds.[1] I strategically chose two top-performing "former Model-C" schools: schools that were reserved for whites during apartheid and desegregated during the transition to democracy.[2] Top-performing former Model-C schools tend to be the most racially and socioeconomically diverse schools in the country.[3] In many ways they are a microcosm of the promises of the post-apartheid moment. They embody the ideals of racial diversity, Rainbow Nationalism, and the possibility for upward mobility. As such, they are often presented as "an important testing ground for new ideas in the battle for transformation" and as "sites of excellent practice where many of the goals of the

METHODOLOGICAL APPENDIX

South African nation can be realized."[4] Although several studies have documented how these schools fail to realize these promises,[5] they remain important spaces that represent the aspirations of racial integration and reconciliation in the new South Africa. I chose such schools because they allowed me to study how histories of racial oppression are engaged in contexts of diversity.[6]

Glenville and Roxbridge High are two of the top-performing schools in the country based on standardized matriculation tests. They are precisely the type of school that is held up as an ideal for public education in post-apartheid South Africa, because of both their high academic standards and their racial diversity. I chose them from a list of top 10 feeder schools into one of the oldest and most prestigious universities in the country. Still, there were important differences between the schools.

While both schools are racially and socioeconomically diverse, the composition of their student bodies differs due to zoning differences and neighborhood demographics. In the post-apartheid era, many Indian families have, for instance, moved into Glenville's previously whites-only neighborhood. Approximately 60 percent of students at Glenville are African. Many of these students commute from a neighboring township in the school's zoning district.[7] Others come from middle- or upper-middle-class families in the neighborhood. A third group are the children of domestic workers in the neighborhood.[8] Whites and Coloureds are in the minority at Glenville High.

Roxbridge High is also located in an area zoned for whites during apartheid, and it has remained predominantly white following the transition to democracy. African students are the second largest group in the school, after whites. Coloureds and

METHODOLOGICAL APPENDIX

TABLE A.1 Schools by race of students (percentages)

	African	Coloured	Indian	White
Glenville High	60	5	30	5
Roxbridge High	40	5	5	50

Note: Figures for Roxbridge High are estimated from Grade 9 class lists. Figures for Glenville High are estimated by the head of the history department.

Indians are in the minority at Roxbridge. Table A.1 summarizes the demographics of the schools by race.

The teaching staff in both schools was predominantly white, as is often the case in former Model-C schools,[9] though this was more so at Roxbridge than Glenville. Table A.2 shows the

TABLE A.2 Characteristics of teachers

Teacher	School	Race	Age
Mr. Lane	Glenville	White	53
Ms. Mokoena	Glenville	African	41
Ms. Ndlovu	Glenville	African	39
Ms. Prescott	Glenville	White	25
Mr. Pretorius	Glenville	White	26
Ms. Devin	Roxbridge	White	25
Ms. Green	Roxbridge	White	26
Ms. Lesley	Roxbridge	White	34
Ms. Roux	Roxbridge	White	27
Ms. Viljoen	Roxbridge	White	42

METHODOLOGICAL APPENDIX

demographics of the Grade 9 history teachers at both schools (all of whom were interviewed for this study). At Roxbridge, all were white, and at Glenville, three were white and two were black African.

English was the medium of instruction at both schools, though half the teachers I interviewed were not first-language English-speakers. When it came to the languages offered at each (the implications of which I explore in chapter 4), Roxbridge offered only Afrikaans as an "additional language" (to English), while Glenville's students chose between Afrikaans and isiZulu.[10]

I focused my study on Grade 9 because this is the year when South African students across the country learn about apartheid in a formal and systematic way in the context of the mandated social sciences curriculum (which is divided between history and geography)—though, as I explain in chapter 2, many had in fact already encountered aspects of apartheid history in earlier grades. At the end of Grade 9, students choose their matriculation subjects—those they'll study through Grade 12. Many choose to drop history as a school subject at that point. At that important moment, students can also elect to leave school completely. Thus Grade 9 may be the last time many students learn history in a formal educational context.

Further, ninth-graders (typically young people aged fourteen and fifteen) are at an important point in their own lives, when lessons learned about "us" and "them," and about history and politics, are highly salient. As Mannheim explains, political experiences and messages encountered during adolescence remain disproportionately influential throughout the life course.[11]

METHODOLOGICAL APPENDIX

This fact is supported by psychological literature, which identifies the same period as key to individuals' consolidation of their own senses of identity.[12]

I negotiated access by first contacting both schools through formal channels for general inquiries, and then by working with the heads of the history departments.

DATA COLLECTION

I embedded myself for fieldwork at Glenville High in 2010 and, the following year, at Roxbridge.[13] My data collection strategy was similar in both sites, though logistical issues led to minor divergences. In the following paragraphs, I describe my three primary data sources: written materials, classroom observations, and in-depth interviews.

WRITTEN MATERIALS

I collected all handouts distributed in class for the apartheid section, as well as for other sections taught during the year. At Glenville, I also collected the notes used in Grades 11 and 12, when those who elect history as a matriculation subject repeat, in greater detail, the sections on apartheid and the Truth and Reconciliation Commission. At Roxbridge, where teachers used a textbook produced by Oxford University Press for Grades 11 and 12, I secured the text through a local bookstore. Finally, I obtained copies of the Revised National Curriculum Statement (RNCS) and the Curriculum and Assessment Policy

METHODOLOGICAL APPENDIX

Statement (CAPS) from contacts at the School of Education at a local university.

Informal conversations with art history teachers in both schools revealed that their curricula include sections on "resistance art," and so I collected handouts on this topic. At Roxbridge, I also collected notes distributed through the life orientation department, which dealt with bullying, racism, and multiculturalism.[14] While these supplementary materials informed my thinking about the project, I only formally analyzed the written materials for Grade 9 history.

OBSERVATIONS

My formal classroom observations tallied approximately four hundred hours, as I conducted daily observations in Grade 9 classes for the duration of the apartheid section (five months of daily observations in seventeen distinct history classes).[15] During my formal observations, I usually sat at the back of the classroom and typed notes on my laptop. In taking my notes, I tried to capture—verbatim—everything said by teachers and students. I also took notes on things that I observed as students were entering and exiting classrooms and on thoughts I had about what was occurring in classrooms.

I supplemented my formal observation of history classes in several ways. While I was at Roxbridge, I participated in optional, school-organized weekend tours of sites of historical interest (the Apartheid Museum, Constitution Hill, and various mnemonic sites in Soweto). Then, in 2012, after I had concluded my research in schools, I observed two teacher workshops. One

METHODOLOGICAL APPENDIX

was for student teachers and covered how to teach the history of the Truth and Reconciliation Commission, while the other was for teachers and focused on how to teach the topic of race. The former was part of the training for a postgraduate diploma in education at a local university. The latter was a collaboration among the same university, the Gauteng Department of Education,[16] and several third-sector organizations.

IN-DEPTH INTERVIEWS

I interviewed all Grade 9 history educators in both schools ($N = 10$). Interviews at both schools were open-ended and semistructured, with a focus on instructors' experiences teaching in post-apartheid classrooms and particularly in teaching the apartheid module. My interview protocol varied slightly between schools. For example, at Roxbridge, the second school I observed, I asked teachers for their opinions on classroom exercises I had observed at Glenville the prior year (see chapter 4). At each school, I asked history department heads specific questions about curriculum structure. At Glenville, I additionally asked the department head about students' interest in Grade 9 history; at Roxbridge, having realized the significance of the comparisons Glenville students made between the Holocaust and apartheid units, I asked this question of all teachers as well (see chapter 2).

I also interviewed 160 students, 82 prior to their exposure to the apartheid section in school (I refer to these students as the "pre" sample) and the balance after that unit (the "post" sample). I randomly sampled students from class registers stratified by race. At Glenville, these were official class lists sorted by race by the head of the history department; at Roxbridge, I was given a spreadsheet of all the Grade 9 students with the racial categorizations provided by their parents or guardians. Additionally, I asked all student interviewees how they identify racially. Most students identified as they had been categorized and used one of apartheid's four official racial categories: African (or black African), Coloured, Indian (or Asian), and white. These categories remain broadly salient in post-apartheid South Africa.[17] Table A.3 presents the characteristics of the student sample using students' own racial identifications given in interviews.[18]

TABLE A.3 Characteristics of students

	Glenville	Roxbridge	Total
Pre-sample			
African	14	8	22
Biracial/Mixed	3	0	3
Coloured	11	8	19
Indian	13	8	21
White	10	7	17
Total	51	31	82
Post-sample			
African	14	10	24
Biracial/Mixed	2	0	2
Coloured	8	10	18
Indian	7	9	16
White	6	12	18
Total	37	41	78
Total	88	72	160

METHODOLOGICAL APPENDIX

At Glenville High, I interviewed the pre-sample in the first two terms of the school year. I then observed during the apartheid section, and I interviewed the post-sample toward the end of the school year. I hoped to repeat this strategy at Roxbridge the following year. However, as I discuss in chapter 2, when I secured access to Roxbridge High at the end of 2010, I was told that students would begin the school year in 2011 with the apartheid section and would spend the rest of the year studying World War II and the Holocaust.[19] This meant that it would be impossible to repeat my research design from Glenville. Therefore, at Roxbridge, I chose to observe during the first term, interview the post-sample in the second term, and then sample from eighth-grade class lists for my third-term pre-sample. The fact that the pre-sample at Glenville resembled the pre-sample at Roxbridge, as did the post-samples in both schools,[20] leads me to believe that cohort dynamics played, if any, a small role in shaping my data. The data were further aligned by the fact that I interviewed Roxbridge's Grade 8 pre-sample toward the *end* of the school year, while I interviewed Glenville's Grade 9 pre-sample toward the *beginning* of the school year. This timing meant that students in both these samples were more or less the same age at the time of their interviews.

Because there were very few whites and Coloureds at Glenville in general, and in the 2010 Grade 9 cohort in particular, these groups were underrepresented in my sample. Thus, in 2011, I returned to conduct twelve more interviews with Glenville ninth-graders (who would have been in Grade 8 in 2010, when I did the bulk of my fieldwork at their school). Eight of these interviews were with white students and four with Coloured students. These students are included in the overall interview count reported in table A.3.

I am often asked why I did not reinterview students in the "pre" sample for the "post" sample. As it turned out, this was not logistically possible at Roxbridge (because, as discussed previously and in chapter 2, the structure of the curriculum meant that I had to interview the "pre" sample *after* I interviewed the "post" sample). But interviewing the same students was never my plan because my interview schedule was essentially the same for both samples and I was concerned that, should I reinterview students within such a short time frame, students would try to be consistent in how they had answered questions in their first interview. Because I sampled randomly from class lists and because I had a relatively high response rate (82.5 percent), I do not believe that there were baseline differences between the two samples. In other words, I believe that the "pre" sample was not systematically different from the "post" sample and the two are therefore comparable, with the key difference being their exposure to the apartheid module in school.

Interviews with students were open-ended and semistructured. My questions aimed to tap into experiences and understandings of race and racism inside and outside of school, knowledge and understanding of apartheid history, and—for students in the post-sample—experiences of history education at school. Student and teacher interviews lasted approximately one hour each. All interviews were recorded and transcribed.

METHODOLOGICAL APPENDIX

DATA ANALYSIS

Data analysis followed a version of the procedures outlined by Deterding and Waters,[21] using the qualitative data analysis software Atlas.ti. In the first round of coding, I engaged in a type of "index coding" combined with a focus on descriptive codes.[22] That is, I coded large chunks of data using the topics I had identified in my semistructured interview protocol, while also inductively developing descriptive codes that I applied to smaller chunks of data. I wrote extensive memos about emerging themes. In the second round of coding, I applied analytic codes developed from the first round of analysis and approached the data with specific questions in mind.

The analysis in chapter 2 is the result of approaching the data with the following question that emerged during the first round of coding: Why is apartheid being framed as "boring" relative to the Holocaust? I coded the data looking for similarities and differences in how these two topics were approached and discussed in written materials, formal lessons, and interviews.

Although my analysis resulted in hundreds of codes, the data presented in chapter 3 are primarily based on the following descriptive codes: "WHITES_AP" and "RESISTANCE_AP." The former refers to discussions of what life was like for whites during apartheid. The latter refers to conversations about resistance to apartheid. I developed the analytic code "BOTH SIDES OF THE STORY" inductively during the process of writing memos around these descriptive codes.

For chapter 4, I began by summarizing how apartheid simulation exercises worked in each Glenville teacher's classrooms.

METHODOLOGICAL APPENDIX

I looked for patterns within and between classrooms, and later, I analyzed how teachers from Roxbridge reacted to my descriptions of the Glenville simulations.

Data presented in chapter 5 are the result of a first round of analysis focused on how students explained contemporary issues in society. A second round of analysis identified whether and how they deployed the past as part of their explanation.

POSITIONALITY

Qualitative researchers have long acknowledged the relational nature of data collection and worked to think through their impact on the field of study.[23] As I discuss at various points in this book, I am a white woman, roughly the same age as many of the teachers at the schools. These aspects of my identity mattered in various ways. On the one hand, my presence in schools and classrooms was not unusual. Both schools were used to having preservice teachers and supervisors present as classroom observers; I easily could have been viewed as one of them. On the other hand, that assumption meant that the students I spoke with likely viewed me as a white authority figure. Students seemed to trust me—several confirmed that our interviews were confidential and then shared things about friends and teachers they wouldn't want attached to their names—but I noted that black students, in particular, did a lot of work in their interviews to explain away apparently racist incidents that had happened at school. I can only imagine that they did this

METHODOLOGICAL APPENDIX

because they believed it was what I—a white woman in a school context—*wanted* to hear.

The resulting data tell us, therefore, not necessarily what students think (information researchers can never really access—we rely on participants' reports) or how they discuss these issues with friends or family. Instead, these data reflect how students think they are *supposed* to talk about race within their desegregated schools. And it is precisely this type of information that helps us understand the ongoing operation of color-blind racism in such schools.

NOTES

1. REMAKING RACE AND NATION THROUGH HISTORY EDUCATION

1. Names of students, teachers, schools, and classrooms are pseudonyms.
2. South African social science tends to divide the population using apartheid racial categories, and these remain salient in how individuals self-identify. These are: African (or black African), Coloured, Indian (or Asian), and white. Echoing anti-apartheid resistance movements, when I use the term "black," I refer inclusively to Africans, Coloureds, and Indians, and in contrast to whites. When respondents in my study used the term "black," they tended to refer to black Africans only. I maintain their terminology in direct quotations and fieldnote extracts.
3. For more on the Rainbow Nation imagery, see Peace Kiguwa, "The Rainbow Nation: Constructs of National Identity in Post-Apartheid South Africa," in *A Race Against Time: Psychology and Challenges to Deracialisation in South Africa*, ed. Garth Stevens, Vijé Franchi, and Tanya Swart (Pretoria: University of South Africa, 2006), 317–34.
4. This depiction is not factually true. There are indeed libraries in Soweto, although Soweto is undeniably more impoverished than is Glenville.
5. For an overview of inequality in South Africa, see the World Bank country overview: https://www.worldbank.org/en/country/southafrica/overview.

1. REMAKING RACE AND NATION THROUGH HISTORY EDUCATION

6. This aggregate fact is true even though intraracial inequality has grown as a share of overall inequality since the transition to democracy; see Jeremy Seekings and Nicoli Nattrass, *Class, Race, and Inequality in South Africa* (New Haven, CT: Yale University Press, 2008).
7. Figures are from Statistics South Africa. For poverty figures, see http://www.statssa.gov.za/publications/Report-03-10-02%20/Report-03-10-02%202015.pdf. For employment figures, see https://www.statssa.gov.za/presentation/Stats%20SA%20presentation%20on%20skills%20and%20unemployment_16%20September.pdf. As with all inequality figures in contemporary South Africa, these figures continue to map onto the apartheid racial hierarchy, with whites at the top of the distribution, black Africans at the bottom, and Indians and Coloureds in the middle—with the latter doing worse than the former.
8. Eduardo Bonilla-Silva, *Racism Without Racists: Color-Blind Racism and the Persistence of Racial Inequality in America*, 6th ed. (Lanham, MD: Rowman & Littlefield, 2021).
9. On the history of segregation and apartheid in South Africa, including ideologies and practices of "separate development," see Harold Wolpe, "Capitalism and Cheap Labour-Power in South Africa: From Segregation to Apartheid," *Economy and Society* 1, no. 4 (1972): 425–56.
10. Bonilla-Silva, *Racism Without Racists*.
11. But see, for example, Hagerman for work on how white children are socialized into color-blindness: Margaret A. Hagerman, *White Kids: Growing Up with Privilege in a Racially Divided America* (New York: New York University Press, 2018); Margaret A. Hagerman, "White Families and Race: Colour-Blind and Colour-Conscious Approaches to White Racial Socialization," *Ethnic and Racial Studies* 37, no. 14 (2014): 2598–614.
12. Eduardo Bonilla-Silva, "More than Prejudice: Restatement, Reflections, and New Directions in Critical Race Theory," *Sociology of Race and Ethnicity* 1, no. 1 (2015): 73–87.
13. Graeme Simpson explains the concept of *ubuntu* as follows: "Ubuntu is the mainspring of the African humanist world-view, an attitude of tolerance and empathy grounded in the interdependence of the individual and the collective. It is conveyed in the expression: '*Motho ke motho ka batho babang*—A person is a person through other people.'" Graeme Simpson, "Tell No Lies, Claim No Easy Victories: A Brief Evaluation of South Africa's Truth and Reconciliation Commission," in *Commissioning the Past: Understanding South Africa's Truth and Reconciliation Commission*,

1. REMAKING RACE AND NATION THROUGH HISTORY EDUCATION

ed. D. Posel and G. Simpson (Johannesburg: Witwatersrand University Press, 2002), 248.

14. The assassination of Chris Hani in 1993 is often considered a watershed moment that threatened to derail the negotiations process and that was contained by Mandela's call for restraint. Hani was leader of the South African Communist Party and chief of staff of *uMkhonto we Sizwe*, the armed wing of the African National Congress (ANC). It is largely believed that, had he not been killed, he would have taken over after Mandela and become the country's second democratically elected president instead of Thabo Mbeki. For an overview of the meaning of Hani's assassination and Mandela's response to it, see Kenneth S. Zagacki, "Rhetoric, Dialogue, and Performance in Nelson Mandela's 'Televised Address on the Assassination of Chris Hani,'" *Rhetoric and Public Affairs* 6, no. 4 (2003): 709–35.

15. This violence was between supporters of the ANC, who were leading the negotiations with the outgoing apartheid regime, and supporters of Inkatha, who opposed the negotiation process until the very last minute. Indeed, Inkatha agreed to participate in the 1994 elections only once the ballot papers had all been printed. Each ballot paper was then appended with a sticker showing the IFP (Inkatha Freedom Party) so that it could be part of the first democratic election. The ANC has traditionally drawn its support base from Xhosa speakers, while the IFP has done so from Zulu speakers.

16. See Stephen Ellis, "The Historical Significance of South Africa's Third Force," *Journal of Southern African Studies* 24, no. 2 (1998): 261–99.

17. Other compromises had to do with the protection of private property rights (which allowed whites to keep their wealth) and the power-sharing arrangements that meant that apartheid-era civil servants kept their jobs in the new dispensation.

18. Under conditions of blanket amnesty, all perpetrators of human rights violations are automatically deemed free from the threat of persecution. Under conditions of individual amnesty, perpetrators have to confess their crimes and show that these were politically motivated in order to be pardoned. On the association between amnesty and amnesia, see Richard Goldstone, "Forward," in *Looking Back, Reaching Forward: Reflections on the Truth and Reconciliation Commission of South Africa*, ed. C. Villa-Vicencio and W. Verwoerd (Cape Town: University of Cape Town Press, 2000), viii–xiii; Priscilla Hayner, "Same Species, Different

1. REMAKING RACE AND NATION THROUGH HISTORY EDUCATION

Animal: How South Africa Compares to Truth Commissions Worldwide," in *Looking Back, Reaching Forward*, 32–41; and Lorna McGregor, "Individual Accountability in South Africa: Cultural Optimum or Political Façade?," *American Journal of International Law* 95, no. 1 (2001): 32–45.

19. For overviews of this argument, see Goldstone, "Forward," viii–xiii; Martha Minow, "Between Vengeance and Forgiveness: South Africa's Truth and Reconciliation Commission," *Negotiation Journal* 14, no. 4 (1998): 319–55; and Jeffrey K. Olick, *The Politics of Regret: On Collective Memory and Historical Responsibility* (New York: Routledge, 2007).

20. Mahmood Mamdani, "A Diminished Truth," *Siyaya!* 3 (1998): 38–41, 40. See also Minow, "Between Vengeance and Forgiveness"; and Deborah Posel, "The TRC Report: What Kind of History? What Kind of Truth?," in *Commissioning the Past*, 147–72.

21. In its final report, the commission argued that although a "just war" had been fought, "unjust means" had sometimes been used. On the "just war" debate, see Richard A. Wilson, *The Politics of Truth and Reconciliation in South Africa: Legitimizing the Post-Apartheid State* (Cambridge: Cambridge University Press, 2001).

22. Benedict Anderson, *Imagined Communities: Reflections on the Origin and Spread of Nationalism* (London: Verso, 2006).

23. Wilson, *The Politics of Truth and Reconciliation in South Africa*, 111.

24. In many ways, this nation-building narrative reflects what scholars of autobiographical accounts call a "conversion narrative." Such narratives involve a story of self-transformation or awakening that works to reconstitute an actor's identity. See Thomas DeGloma, "Awakenings: Autobiography, Memory, and the Social Logic of Personal Discovery," *Sociological Forum* 25, no. 3 (2010): 519–40; Thomas DeGloma, *Seeing the Light: The Social Logic of Personal Discovery* (Chicago: University of Chicago Press, 2014); David Flores, "From Prowar Soldier to Antiwar Activist: Change and Continuity in the Narratives of Political Conversion Among Iraq War Veterans," *Symbolic Interaction* 39, no. 2 (2016): 196–212; and Douglas Schrock, Janice McCabe, and Christian Vaccaro, "Narrative Manhood Acts: Batterer Intervention Program Graduates' Tragic Relationships," *Symbolic Interaction* 41, no. 3 (2018): 384–410.

25. James L. Gibson, "Does Truth Lead to Reconciliation? Testing the Causal Assumptions of the South African Truth and Reconciliation Process," *American Journal of Political Science* 48, no. 2 (2004): 201–17. Reconciliation was measured as inter-racial trust, support for

new democratic institutions, political tolerance, and support for human rights.

26. This point is clearly exemplified by the rise of the Economic Freedom Fighters (EFF)—a political party campaigning, among other things, on policies of land redistribution—which won over 6 percent of the vote in the 2014 general election and over 10 percent in the 2019 one. It is also exemplified by the Rhodes Must Fall and Fees Must Fall movements on university campuses that began in 2015. See conclusion for further discussion.

27. Amanda E. Lewis, *Race in the Schoolyard: Negotiating the Color Line in Classrooms and Communities* (New Brunswick, NJ: Rutgers University Press, 2003), 4.

28. See Michael Apple, *Ideology and Curriculum* (Abingdon, UK: Routledge, 2004); Samuel Bowles and Herbert Gintis, *Schooling in Capitalist America: Educational Reform and the Contradictions of Economic Life* (Chicago: Haymarket, 2011).

29. Amanda E. Lewis and John B. Diamond, *Despite the Best Intentions: How Racial Inequality Thrives in Good Schools* (Oxford: Oxford University Press, 2015).

30. Mica Pollock, *Colormute: Race Talk Dilemmas in an American School* (Princeton, NJ: Princeton University Press, 2009).

31. Karolyn Tyson, *Integration Interrupted: Tracking, Black Students, and Acting White After Brown* (Oxford: Oxford University Press, 2011). See also Lewis and Diamond, *Despite the Best Intentions*.

32. Edward W. Morris, "'Tuck in That Shirt!' Race, Class, Gender, and Discipline in an Urban School," *Sociological Perspectives* 48, no. 1 (2005): 25–48. See also Lewis and Diamond, *Despite the Best Intentions*.

33. Jessica McCrory Calarco, "Coached for the Classroom: Parents' Cultural Transmission and Children's Reproduction of Educational Inequalities," *American Sociological Review* 79, no. 5 (2014): 1015–37; Prudence L. Carter, *Keepin' it Real: School Success Beyond Black and White* (Oxford: Oxford University Press, 2005); Mark Hunter, *Race for Education: Gender, White Tone, and Schooling in South Africa* (Cambridge: Cambridge University Press, 2019); Annette Lareau, "Social Class Differences in Family-School Relationships: The Importance of Cultural Capital," *Sociology of Education* 60, no. 2 (1987): 73–85; Natasha Warikoo, "Addressing Emotional Health While Protecting Status: Asian American and White Parents in Suburban America," *American Journal of Sociology* 126, no. 3 (2020): 545–76.

1. REMAKING RACE AND NATION THROUGH HISTORY EDUCATION

34. Prudence L. Carter, *Stubborn Roots: Race, Culture, and Inequality in U.S. and South African Schools* (Oxford: Oxford University Press, 2012). For further discussion of how material disparities lead to distributional inequality while sociocultural ones lead to relational inequality and how both of these dimensions lead to "unrealized integration" in educational spaces, see Prudence L. Carter, "Unrealized Integration in Education, Sociology, and Society," *American Sociological Review* 89, no. 1 (2024): 6–30.
35. In a study of schooling in eThekwini in South Africa, Hunter (*Race for Education*) incisively documents how desegregated South African schools have maintained their "white tone," using the presence of phenotypically white students as well as white cultural practices (e.g., sports historically coded as "white") as markers of prestige in the post-apartheid era.
36. Of course, history curricula and textbooks can and often do exclude such discussions; see J. A. Banks, "Approaches to Multicultural Curriculum Reform," *Trotter Review* 3, no. 3 (1989): 17–19; and Melissa F. Weiner, "(E)RACING SLAVERY: Racial Neoliberalism, Social Forgetting, and Scientific Colonialism in Dutch Primary School History Textbooks," *Du Bois Review: Social Science Research on Race* 11, no. 2 (2014): 329–51.
37. John S. Willis, "Who Needs Multicultural Education? White Students, U.S. History, and the Construction of a Usable Past," *Anthropology and Education Quarterly* 27, no. 3 (1996): 365–89.
38. On the challenge of being "forced to remember," see Vered Vinitzky-Seroussi, *Yitzhak Rabin's Assassination and the Dilemmas of Commemoration* (Albany, NY: State University of New York Press, 2010); Vered Vinitzky-Seroussi and Chana Teeger, "Unpacking the Unspoken: Silence in Collective Memory and Forgetting," *Social Forces* 88, no. 3 (2010): 1103–22; and Vered Vinitzky-Seroussi and Chana Teeger, "Silence and Collective Memory," in *Oxford Handbook of Cognitive Sociology*, ed. W. H. Brekhaus and G. Ignatow (New York: Oxford University Press, 2019), 663–74.
39. Banks, "Approaches to Multicultural Curriculum Reform," 17–19; Tamara Pavasović Trošt, "Ruptures and Continuities in Nationhood Narratives: Reconstructing the Nation Through History Textbooks in Serbia and Croatia," *Nations and Nationalism* 24, no. 3 (2018): 716–40; Tamara Trošt, "History Textbooks and Transitional Justice," in *The Oxford Handbook of Transitional Justice*, ed. J. Meierhenrich, A. Laban Hinton, and L. Douglas (New York: Oxford University Press, 2023).

40. Banks, "Approaches to Multicultural Curriculum Reform," 17.
41. Terrie Epstein, *Interpreting National History: Race, Identity, and Pedagogy in Classrooms and Communities* (Abingdon, UK: Routledge, 2010).
42. These boundaries are examples of what Lamont and Molnár call "symbolic boundaries," namely, "conceptual distinctions made by social actors to categorize objects, people, practices, and even time and space." See Michèle Lamont and Virág Molnár, "The Study of Boundaries in the Social Sciences," *Annual Review of Sociology* 28, no. 1 (2002): 168. See also Wagner-Pacifici for a discussion of the role of "collective shifters like 'we' and 'they'" in constituting historical transitions and events more generally: Robin Wagner-Pacifici, "Theorizing the Restlessness of Events," *American Journal of Sociology* 115, no. 5 (2010): 1360.
43. Scholars of identity have long noted that individual behavior is guided both by our internally held sense of identity and by the expectations that are placed on us in particular contexts populated by particular kinds of people. See, for example, Rogers Brubaker and Frederick Cooper, "Beyond 'Identity,'" *Theory and Society* 29, no. 1 (2000): 1–47; and Sheldon Stryker and Peter J. Burke, "The Past, Present, and Future of an Identity Theory," *Social Psychology Quarterly* 63, no. 4 (2000): 284–97. Researchers have taken heed of this dynamic by thinking through issues of research positionality; see for example Victoria Reyes, "Ethnographic Toolkit: Strategic Positionality and Researchers' Visible and Invisible Tools in Field Research," *Ethnography* 21, no. 2 (2020): 220–40.
44. Fees at both schools were approximately 40,000 ZAR per year in 2019 (3,500 USD). Private school fees would have been approximately 140,000 ZAR (10,000 USD) per year.
45. Graeme Bloch, *The Toxic Mix: What's Wrong with South Africa's Schools and How to Fix It* (Cape Town: Tafelberg, 2009); Carter, *Stubborn Roots*.
46. In the methodological appendix, I also provide further detail on my research design and data collection and analysis procedures, including the supplementary information I gathered by participating in school trips and teacher training workshops.
47. This focus on the institutional contexts in which individuals learn about the past brings together two strands in the collective memory literature. First, at the level of what Jeffrey Olick calls "collective memory," researchers have documented how national and other group pasts are represented in museums, monuments, truth commissions, and official texts and proclamations. See Jeffrey K. Olick, "Collective Memory: The Two Cultures,"

1. REMAKING RACE AND NATION THROUGH HISTORY EDUCATION

Sociological Theory 17, no. 3 (1999): 333–48. For examples of research in this tradition, see Jeffrey K. Olick, *In the House of the Hangman: The Agonies of German Defeat, 1943–1949* (Chicago: University of Chicago Press, 2005); Christina Simko, *The Politics of Consolation: Memory and the Meaning of September 11* (Oxford: Oxford University Press, 2015); Vered Vinitzky-Seroussi, "Commemorating a Difficult Past: Yitzhak Rabin's Memorials," *American Sociological Review* (2002): 30–51; and Vera L. Zolberg, "Museums as Contested Sites of Remembrance: The Enola Gay Affair," *Sociological Review* 43, no. S1 (1995): 69–82. Second, there is also what Olick explains as the level of "collected memories": how individuals remember their national, ethnic, and other group pasts (Olick, "Collective Memory"). For examples of research in this tradition, see Luisa Passerini, *Fascism in Popular Memory: The Cultural Experience of the Turin Working Class* (Cambridge: Cambridge University Press, 1987); Howard Schuman and Jacqueline Scott, "Generations and Collective Memories," *American Sociological Review* 54, no. 3 (1989): 359–81; and Howard Schuman, Vered Vinitzky-Seroussi, and Amiram D. Vinokur, "Keeping the Past Alive: Memories of Israeli Jews at the Turn of the Millennium," *Sociological Forum* 18, no. 1 (2003): 103–36. We know much less about the connections between these two levels. This book addresses this gap by focusing on schools as spaces where institutionalized versions of the past are transmitted to individuals in face-to-face settings.

48. See P. R. Lockhart, "Schools Keep Teaching Slavery and Civil Rights History in Ways That Traumatize Black Students," VOX, April 19, 2019, https://www.vox.com/identities/2019/4/19/18507873/arizona-school-segregation-lesson-slavery-civil-rights-history.

2. JUXTAPOSITIONS

1. I discuss how I dealt with this issue in the methodological appendix.
2. Gail Weldon, "Memory, Identity and the Politics of Curriculum Construction in Transition Societies: Rwanda and South Africa," *Perspectives in Education* 27, no. 2 (2009): 177–89.
3. See Weldon, "Memory, Identity and the Politics of Curriculum Construction."
4. Linda Chisholm, "The State of Curriculum Reform in South Africa: The Issue of Curriculum 2005," in *State of the Nation: South Africa 2003–2004*, ed. J. Daniel, A. Habib, and R. Southall (Cape Town: HSRC Press, 2003), 268–89.

2. JUXTAPOSITIONS

5. See Weldon, "Memory, Identity and the Politics of Curriculum Construction."
6. Revised National Curriculum Statement, Grades 7–9 (Schools) Senior Phase, (Pretoria: Department of Education, 2004), 2.
7. Revised National Curriculum Statement, Grades 7–9, 11.
8. Revised National Curriculum Statement, Teacher's Guide (Pretoria: Department of Education, 2003), 19.
9. For a study on the development of a thematic focus in the South African history curriculum, see Carol Bertram, "The Recontextualising Logics of Four Post-Colonial African School History Curriculum Documents: Kenya, Rwanda, South Africa and Zimbabwe," in *Teaching African History in Schools*, ed. Denise Bentrovato and Johan Wassermann, (Boston: Brill, 2021) 15–44.
10. For a discussion of how the Holocaust is used as a "bridge" for understanding human rights abuses during apartheid, see Natasha Robinson "Using Holocaust Education as a 'Bridge' to Learning about Apartheid in a South African History Classroom: The Development of 'Interpretive frames' through Comparative Histories," *Holocaust and Genocide Studies* (forthcoming).
11. A new curriculum brought into effect shortly after conclusion of my fieldwork solidified this juxtaposition by removing all topics aside from the Holocaust and apartheid from the Grade 9 history curriculum. A short section (recommended to last two hours) on the nature of race was also added. This new curriculum was called the Curriculum and Assessment Policy Statement (CAPS), and it was still in effect at the time of writing. For a discussion of how South African students are learning about "the definition of race," see Natasha Robinson and Nicholas Kerswill, "'Myth' or 'Construct'?: What Students are Learning about Race in the South African History Classroom," *Yesterday and Today* 29, no. 1 (2023): 52–71.
12. In many ways, this narrative fits into the classical melodrama genre in which there is a clear villain, clear victims, and a clear definition of good and evil; see Donileen R. Loseke, "Examining Emotion as Discourse: Emotion Codes and Presidential Speeches Justifying War," *Sociological Quarterly* 50, no. 3 (2009): 497–524.
13. Eviatar Zerubavel, "In the Beginning: Notes on the Social Construction of Historical Discontinuity," *Sociological Inquiry* 63, no. 4 (1993): 457–59.
14. See, for example, Michael Burawoy, "The Capitalist State in South Africa: Marxist and Sociological Perspectives on Race and Class," *Political Power and Social Theory* 2 (1981): 279–335; Anthony W. Marx, *Making*

2. JUXTAPOSITIONS

Race and Nation: A Comparison of South Africa, the United States, and Brazil (Cambridge: Cambridge University Press, 1998); and Harold Wolpe, "Capitalism and Cheap Labour-Power in South Africa: From Segregation to Apartheid," *Economy and Society* 1, no. 4 (1972): 425–56.

15. These were the same in both schools. The events included the Defiance Campaign, the Freedom Charter, the Sharpeville Massacre, the Soweto Uprising, and the Women's March. The resistance organizations included the African National Congress, the Pan Africanist Congress, and the Black Consciousness Movement.

16. As discussed further in the methodological appendix, I report on participants' race as they identified themselves to me in interviews. Most students identified using one of apartheid's official racial categories. However, five identified as biracial (or mixed), possibly reflecting the emergence of new racial categories in post-apartheid South Africa. While the term Coloured is often understood to refer to people of mixed-racial backgrounds, the five students who identified as biracial/mixed explained that to be Coloured, one's parents would also have to be Coloured. In contrast, they explained that they identified as biracial because they came from an interracial family. On the meaning of Coloured identity and the historical construction of this distinct racial category in South Africa, see Zimitri Erasmus, *Coloured by History, Shaped by Place: New Perspectives on Coloured Identities in Cape Town* (Cape Town: Kwela, 2001); Whitney N. Laster Pirtle, "'White People Still Come Out on Top': The Persistence of White Supremacy in Shaping Coloured South Africans' Perceptions of Racial Hierarchy and Experiences of Racism in Post-Apartheid South Africa," *Social Sciences* 11, no. 2 (2022): 70; and Tessa Dooms and Lynsey Ebony Chutel, *Coloured: How Classification Became Culture* (Johannesburg: Jonathan Ball, 2023).

17. June 16 is now called "Youth Day." For a discussion on the significance of renaming public holidays in South Africa, see Chana Teeger and Vered Vinitzky-Seroussi, "Controlling for Consensus: Commemorating Apartheid in South Africa," *Symbolic Interaction* 30, no. 1 (2007): 57–78.

18. This act dispossessed black Africans of their land, reserving 90 percent of the land in South Africa for whites.

19. For a more expansive historiography that locates the Holocaust in long-standing European anti-Semitism and modernity, see, for example, Zygmunt Bauman, *Modernity and the Holocaust* (Ithaca, NY: Cornell University Press, 2000); and William Brustein, *Roots of Hate: Anti-Semitism in Europe Before the Holocaust* (Cambridge: Cambridge University Press, 2003).

2. JUXTAPOSITIONS

20. Historians refer to this process as "historical consciousness." On the role of causality in historiography, see Edward Hallett Carr, *What Is History?* (Hampshire: Palgrave, 2001); Richard J. Evans, *In Defence of History* (London: Granta, 2012); and Peter Seixas, "A Model of Historical Thinking," *Educational Philosophy and Theory* 49, no. 6 (2017): 593–605. On historical consciousness in history education, see Catherine Duquette, "Relating Historical Consciousness to Historical Thinking Through Assessment," in *New Directions in Assessing Historical Thinking*, ed. Kadriye Ercikan and Peter Seixas, (New York: Routledge, 2015) 51–63; Natasha Robinson, "History Education for Transitional Justice: How Students Understand and Construct Historical Legacies in the Post-Apartheid South African History Classroom" (PhD diss., University of Oxford, 2020); and Natasha Robinson, "Developing Historical Consciousness for Social Cohesion: How South African Students Learn to Construct the Relationship Between Past and Present," in *Historical Justice and History Education*, ed. Matilda Keynes, Henrik Åström Elmersjö, Daniel Lindmark, Björn Norlin, (Cham, Switzerland: Palgrave, 2021) 341–63. On the relationship between causality and "legacy thinking," see Natasha Robinson, "Conceptualising Historical Legacies for Transitional Justice History Education in Postcolonial Societies," *History Education Research Journal* 19, no. 1 (2022): 10.
21. In this way, boredom can be understood as a racialized emotion—that is, an emotion expressed in a racially stratified way and used to reproduce inequality. I elaborate on this idea in Chana Teeger "(Not) Feeling the Past: Boredom as a Racialized Emotion," *American Journal of Sociology* 129, no. 1 (2023): 1–40. For more on racialized emotions, see Eduardo Bonilla-Silva, "Feeling Race: Theorizing the Racial Economy of Emotions," *American Sociological Review* 84, no. 1 (2019): 1–25; Sarah Diefendorf and C. J. Pascoe, "In the Name of Love: White Organizations and Racialized Emotions," *Social Problems* (2023); Nadena Doharty, "The 'Angry Black Woman' as Intellectual Bondage: Being Strategically Emotional on the Academic Plantation," *Race Ethnicity and Education* 23, no. 4 (2020): 548–62; Amy G. Halberstadt et al., "Racialized Emotion Recognition Accuracy and Anger Bias of Children's Faces," *Emotion* 22, no. 3 (2022): 403; Simone Ispa-Landa and Sara Thomas, "Race, Gender, and Emotion Work Among School Principals," *Gender and Society* 33, no. 3 (2019): 387–409; Kiran Mirchandani, "Challenging Racial Silences in Studies of Emotion Work: Contributions from Anti-Racist Feminist Theory," *Organization Studies* 24, no. 5 (2003): 721–42; Jennifer L. Nelson

2. JUXTAPOSITIONS

and Tiffany D. Johnson, "How White Workers Navigate Racial Difference in the Workplace: Social-Emotional Processes and the Role of Workplace Racial Composition," *Work and Occupations* (2023); Amy C. Wilkins and Jennifer A. Pace, "Class, Race, and Emotions," in *Handbook of the Sociology of Emotions: Volume II*, ed. Jan E. Stets and Jonathan H. Turner, (New York: Springer, 2014) 385–409; Adia Harvey Wingfield, "The Modern Mammy and the Angry Black Man: African American Professionals' Experiences with Gendered Racism in the Workplace," *Race, Gender and Class* 14, no. 1–2 (2007): 196–212; and Adia Harvey Wingfield, "Are Some Emotions Marked 'Whites Only'? Racialized Feeling Rules in Professional Workplaces," *Social Problems* 57, no. 2 (2010): 251–68.

22. This boredom is different from that documented by social theorists, who have pointed to boredom as a constitutive—and pervasive—feature of modernity; see, for example, Jack M. Barbalet, "Boredom and Social Meaning," *British Journal of Sociology* 50, no. 4 (1999): 631–46; Dennis Brissett and Robert P. Snow, "Boredom: Where the Future Isn't," *Symbolic Interaction* 16, no. 3 (1993): 237–56; Michael E. Gardiner, "Henri Lefebvre and the 'Sociology of Boredom,'" *Theory, Culture and Society* 29, no. 2 (2012): 37–62; Rasmus Johnsen, "Boredom and Organization Studies," *Organization Studies* 37, no. 10 (2016): 1403–15; and Elina Tochilnikova, *Towards a General Theory of Boredom: A Case Study of Anglo and Russian Society* (New York: Routledge, 2020). It is also different from that described by school ethnographers, who document how young people enact boredom to look "cool" and resist authority; see, for example, Georg Breidenstein, "The Meaning of Boredom in School Lessons: Participant Observation in the Seventh and Eighth Form," *Ethnography and Education* 2, no. 1 (2007): 93–108; and Murray Milner Jr., *Freaks, Geeks, and Cool Kids: American Teenagers, Schools, and the Culture of Consumption* (New York: Routledge, 2013). Instead, students at Roxbridge and Glenville described only part of the school history curriculum as boring (namely, apartheid), while displaying high levels of interest in other parts (namely, the Holocaust).

3. EQUIVALENCES

1. One teacher, Ms. Viljoen, mentioned this fact on one occasion. However, she immediately reminded her students that there were also many whites who were against these policies.

3. EQUIVALENCES

2. On the distinction between interpersonal and structural or institutional racism, see Matthew Desmond and Mustafa Emirbayer, "What Is Racial Domination?," *Du Bois Review: Social Science Research on Race* 6, no. 2 (2009): 335–55; Mary C. Waters, *Black Identities: West Indian Immigrant Dreams and American Realities* (Cambridge, MA: Harvard University Press, 1999); and Chana Teeger "Ruptures in the Rainbow Nation: How Desegregated South African Schools Deal with Interpersonal and Structural Racism," *Sociology of Education* 88, no. 3 (2015): 226–43.
3. For more on the concept of *ubuntu* and how it was mobilized during the time of the TRC, see Graeme Simpson, "Tell No Lies, Claim No Easy Victories: A Brief Evaluation of South Africa's Truth and Reconciliation Commission," in *Commissioning the Past: Understanding South Africa's Truth and Reconciliation Commission*, ed Deborah Posel and Graeme Simpson (Johannesburg: Witwatersrand University Press, 2002); and Richard A. Wilson, *The Politics of Truth and Reconciliation in South Africa: Legitimizing the Post-Apartheid State* (Cambridge: Cambridge University Press, 2001), as well as chapter 1 of this book.
4. Scholars have shown how white supremacy is sustained by whites' commitment to an epistemology of ignorance, that is, "a way of knowing oriented towards evading, mystifying and obscuring the reality of racism"; see Jennifer C. Mueller, "Racial Ideology or Racial Ignorance? An Alternative Theory of Racial Cognition," *Sociological Theory* 38, no. 2 (2020): 147. See also Charles Mills, "White Ignorance," in *Race and Epistemologies of Ignorance*, eds, Shannon Sullivan and Nancy Tuana (Albany: SUNY Press 2007), 13–38 and Melissa Steyn, "The Ignorance Contract: Recollections of Apartheid Childhoods and the Construction of Epistemologies of Ignorance," *Identities* 19, no. 1 (2012): 8–25.
5. The difference was least marked for white students, suggesting that they may have been exposed to this idea at home more than other students.
6. During data analysis, I developed a code to capture the idea that not all whites supported the apartheid system. This idea arose when I asked students directly who suffered during apartheid or what life was like for whites during apartheid. On occasion, it also came up in other parts of the interview. I counted the code only once per student, regardless of where or how many times it was mentioned in the interview.
7. On the ANC's armed resistance, see Chana Teeger and Vered Vinitzky-Seroussi, "Controlling for Consensus: Commemorating Apartheid in South Africa," *Symbolic Interaction* 30, no. 1 (2007): 57–78.

3. EQUIVALENCES

8. Similarly, see Yazdiha for a discussion of how whitewashed versions of Dr. Martin Luther King have been "juxtaposed against memories of 'radical,' 'threatening' activists like Malcolm X and the black Panthers as 'divisive' separatists": Hajar Yazdiha, *The Struggle for the People's King* (Princeton, NJ: Princeton University Press, 2023), 5.
9. As discussed in chapter 1 and the methodological appendix, neither school used textbooks. Instead, both schools independently created and distributed booklets to students for each section covered in history.
10. See, for example, Howard Schuman and Jacqueline Scott, "Generations and Collective Memories," *American Sociological Review* 54, no. 3 (1989): 359–81; and Howard Schuman and Cheryl Rieger, "Historical Analogies, Generational Effects, and Attitudes Toward War," *American Sociological Review* 57, no. 3 (1992): 315–26.
11. See Zembylas for a discussion on the pedagogical value of engaging with, rather than trying to avoid, discomfort in the classroom: Michalinos Zembylas, "'Pedagogy of Discomfort' and Its Ethical Implications: The Tensions of Ethical Violence in Social Justice Education," *Ethics and Education* 10, no. 2 (2015): 163–74.
12. This part of the narrative is similar to one of the storylines of color-blind racism identified in the United States by Eduardo Bonilla-Silva, namely, "I never owned slaves": Eduardo Bonilla-Silva, *Racism Without Racists: Color-Blind Racism and the Persistence of Racial Inequality in America*, 6th ed. (Lanham, MD: Rowman & Littlefield, 2021).
13. Netball is a ball sport (most similar to basketball) played in many former British colonies. It has historically been a "female sport" and is very popular in South African schools.
14. In addition, the seminar was supposed to introduce participants to general teaching techniques that they could use across subject areas. This specific class introduced them to the "academic controversy approach" in which students have to break up into small groups and argue a side of the debate based on readings that they have been assigned. This strategy for teaching contentious issues is interesting in itself because it forces students to debate issues based on a perspective assigned to them, rather than allowing them to debate from their own positions.
15. The Reconstruction and Development Programme outlined the government's economic policies following the transition.

4. SIMULATIONS

16. In the RDP, the government stipulated its policies around the provision of services, including houses. The "RDP houses" that were built are easily identified by their uniform and basic structure.
17. Note that Mike did not identify the race of the student or tutor in this story. However, from the content of the story, combined with his own racial identification at the beginning of the story, it is clear that both the student and the tutor were black. For a discussion of the micro-interactional processes of "race talk" in South Africa, see Kevin A. Whitehead, "'Categorizing the Categorizer': The Management of Racial Common Sense in Interaction," *Social Psychology Quarterly* 72, no. 4 (2009): 325–42.
18. See Ann Swidler, "Culture in Action: Symbols and Strategies," *American Sociological Review* 51, no. 2 (1986): 273–86. Swidler offers "an image of culture as a 'tool-kit' of symbols, stories, rituals, and world views, which people may use in varying configurations to solve different kinds of problems (273)."

4. SIMULATIONS

1. During apartheid, South Africa's official languages were English and Afrikaans. In the democratic era, nine additional indigenous African languages were added as official languages (isiZulu, isiXhosa, Sepedi, Setswana, Sesotho, Xitsonga, Siswati, Tshivenda, and isiNdebele). According to the 2011 census, 96.7 percent of white South Africans speak either English (35.9 percent) or Afrikaans (60.8 percent) as their first language. Coloured South Africans also speak English (20.8 percent) or Afrikaans (75.8 percent) as their first language. English is also spoken as a first language by 86.1 percent of South African Indians/Asians. Only 4.4 percent of black Africans speak English (1.5 percent) or Afrikaans (2.9 percent) as a first language. Aside from South African Sign Language, which became the country's twelfth official language in 2023 (0.5 percent), or another language not listed in the census options (1.5 percent), the rest of the population speaks one of the other nine official languages, with isiZulu (28.5 percent) and isiXhosa (20.1 percent) being the most frequently mentioned.
2. Ms. Prescott and Ms. Ndlovu had Coloureds entering second and Indians third. Ms. Mokoena, who had only Indian, Coloured, and African students in her "Afrikaans class," had them enter in that order: Indian, Coloured, African. Ms. Mokoena's system (save the obvious absence of

4. SIMULATIONS

whites) more accurately reflected the apartheid system's hierarchy than the other two teachers' systems.
3. At the time, Jacob Zuma was president of the Republic of South Africa and Kgalema Motlanthe was deputy president.
4. On the distinction between identification (how we define ourselves) and categorization (how others define us), see Richard Jenkins, "Rethinking Ethnicity: Identity, Categorization and Power," *Ethnic and Racial Studies* 17, no. 2 (1994): 197–223.
5. Homelands, or bantustans, were ethnically designated areas where the majority of black Africans were forced to live during apartheid.
6. Chana Teeger, "Ruptures in the Rainbow Nation: How Desegregated South African Schools Deal with Interpersonal and Structural Racism," *Sociology of Education* 88, no. 3 (2015): 226–43. For a broad discussion of the forms and functions of racist humor, see also Raúl Pérez, *The Souls of White Jokes: How Racist Humor Fuels White Supremacy* (Stanford, CA: Stanford University Press, 2022).
7. Helen Joseph was a white anti-apartheid activist who, under the auspices of the multiracial Federation of South African Women, jointly spearheaded the famous women's march on August 9, 1956, to protest against the pass laws.
8. "Boss" in Afrikaans has a similar connotation to "master."
9. For more information, see South African History Online (http://www.sahistory.org.za).
10. In many ways, teachers' stated objectives echo researchers' findings about the value of "perspective taking" in reducing racial bias. See Marco Brambilla, Marcella Ravenna, and Miles Hewstone, "Changing Stereotype Content Through Mental Imagery: Imagining Intergroup Contact Promotes Stereotype Change," *Group Processes and Intergroup Relations* 15, no. 3 (2012): 305–15; Adam D. Galinsky and Gillian Ku, "The Effects of Perspective-Taking on Prejudice: The Moderating Role of Self-Evaluation," *Personality and Social Psychology Bulletin* 30, no. 5 (2004): 594–604; and Nicole M. Stephens, Lauren A. Rivera, and S. Townsend, "What Works to Increase Diversity? A Multi-Level Approach," *Research in Organizational Behavior* 39 (2020): 1–51. These researchers study a variety of interventions aimed at generating empathy for people in a different social position by asking participants to imagine themselves "in someone else's shoes." However, in Glenville's simulations, students were asked to

4. SIMULATIONS

step back in time, but in their own shoes (occupying their current racial identities, but imagining they were in the past).

11. As the name of the act suggests, the act abolished the various pass laws that were in place across the country's different provinces and created a unified national policy whereby all Africans were required to carry a "reference book" (also referred to as the "pass" or "dompas," literally meaning "dumb pass" in Afrikaans).

12. According to the Revised National Curriculum Statement, social sciences is divided between geography and history. At Roxbridge, students learned both geography and history throughout the school year and were taught by teachers who specialized in each of these subjects. At Glenville, classrooms were allocated either a geography or a history teacher for social sciences in its entirety. The school year was divided into modules, and teachers switched from history to geography and back again every few months. Mr. Lane and Mr. Pretorius were geography teachers. Ms. Prescott, Ms. Ndlovu, and Ms. Mokoena were history teachers.

13. Julius Malema is currently head of the Economic Freedom Fighters political party. I discuss the significance of this party further on in this chapter as well as in chapter 1 and the conclusion.

14. Referring to the multinational mining company, Anglo-American.

15. Ms. Viljoen's depiction of Afrikaans-medium schools as homogenous (by which I understood her to mean white and middle class) would not necessarily apply to other provinces in South Africa, like the Western Cape and the Northern Cape, both of which have large Coloured populations who speak Afrikaans as their first language. For a discussion of young white Afrikaans-speakers' experiences in primarily white, as well as more racially diverse, schools, see Jacob R. Boersema, *Can We Unlearn Racism? What South Africa Teaches Us About Whiteness* (Stanford, CA: Stanford University Press, 2022). For a discussion of the experiences of white Afrikaans-speaking university students, see Jonathan D. Jansen, *Knowledge in the Blood: Confronting Race and the Apartheid Past* (Stanford, CA: Stanford University Press, 2009).

16. In some ways, this idea echoes Jane Elliott's blue eyes/brown eyes experiment. Elliott was an elementary schoolteacher in the United States who, following the assassination of Martin Luther King Jr., devised a role-playing activity to teach her students about prejudice. In this activity, students' eye color (blue or brown) determined how they were treated (unfairly or favorably). For a discussion of this activity, including its

4. SIMULATIONS

ethical implications, see Deborah A. Byrnes and Gary Kiger, "Prejudice-Reduction Simulations: Ethics, Evaluations, and Theory into Practice," *Simulation and Gaming* 23, no. 4 (1992): 457–71.

17. On the construction of collective memory in the Apartheid Museum, see Robyn Autry, *Desegregating the Past: The Public Life of Memory in the United States and South Africa* (New York: Columbia University Press, 2017); and Chana Teeger and Vered Vinitzky-Seroussi, "Controlling for Consensus: Commemorating Apartheid in South Africa," *Symbolic Interaction* 30, no. 1 (2007): 57–78.

18. For more on racial classification during apartheid, see Deborah Posel, "Race as Common Sense: Racial Classification in Twentieth-Century South Africa," *African Studies Review* 44, no. 2 (2001): 87–114.

19. Most South Africans, of course, never came before the Racial Classification Board; they were simply assigned their parents' race.

5. CONSEQUENCES

1. For other examples of studies that examine how individuals use the past to explain contemporary social problems, see Catherine Duquette, "Relating Historical Consciousness to Historical Thinking Through Assessment," in *New Directions in Assessing Historical Thinking*, ed. Kadriye Ercikan and Peter Seixas, (New York: Routledge, 2015) 51–63; Natasha Robinson, "History Education for Transitional Justice: How Students Understand and Construct Historical Legacies in the Post-Apartheid South African History Classroom" (PhD diss., University of Oxford, 2020); Natasha Robinson, "Developing Historical Consciousness for Social Cohesion: How South African Students Learn to Construct the Relationship Between Past and Present," in *Historical Justice and History Education*, ed. Matilda Keynes, Henrik Åström Elmersjö, Daniel Lindmark, Björn Norlin, (Cham, Switzerland: Palgrave, 2021) 341–63; and Chana Teeger, "Collective Memory and Collective Fear: How South Africans Use the Past to Explain Crime," *Qualitative Sociology* 37, no. 1 (2014): 69–92.

2. For an elaboration on this point, see Chana Teeger, "Ruptures in the Rainbow Nation: How Desegregated South African Schools Deal with Interpersonal and Structural Racism," *Sociology of Education* 88, no. 3 (2015): 226–43.

3. See David O. Sears, "Symbolic Racism," in *Eliminating Racism: Profiles in Controversy*, ed. Phyllis A. Katz and Dalmas A. Taylor (New York:

Springer, 1988), 56. See also Donald R. Kinder and David O. Sears, "Prejudice and Politics: Symbolic Racism Versus Racial Threats to the Good Life," *Journal of Personality and Social Psychology* 40, no. 3 (1981): 414–431.
4. Lawrence Bobo, James R. Kluegel, and Ryan A. Smith, "Laissez-Faire Racism: The Crystallization of a Kinder, Gentler, Antiblack Ideology," in *Racial Attitudes in the 1990s: Continuity and Change*, ed. Steven A Tuch and Jack K. Martin (Westport, CT: Praeger, 1997), 23–25. See also Herbert Blumer, "Race Prejudice as a Sense of Group Position," *Pacific Sociological Review* 1, no. 1 (1958): 3–7; and Lawrence Bobo, "Race, Interests, and Beliefs About Affirmative Action: Unanswered Questions and New Directions," *American Behavioral Scientist* 41, no. 7 (1998): 985–1003.
5. Lincoln Quillian, "New Approaches to Understanding Racial Prejudice and Discrimination," *Annual Review of Sociology* 32 (2006): 299–328, 312.
6. Jacob Zuma was president of South Africa during the time the research was conducted.

CONCLUSION

1. The Freedom Charter was adopted in 1955 at the Congress of the People held in Kliptown, Soweto. The document espoused the principles of the Congress Alliance, led by the African National Congress and its allies. The principles were compiled based on submissions made by the people of South Africa.
2. A sport somewhat similar to basketball; see chapter 3, note 13.
3. Graeme Bloch, *The Toxic Mix: What's Wrong with South Africa's Schools and How to Fix It* (Cape Town: Tafelberg, 2009), 148.
4. For a review of scholarship on the role of schools in mediating family background on academic achievement, see Steven Brint, "The 'Collective Mind' at Work: A Decade in the Life of U.S. Sociology of Education," *Sociology of Education* 86, no. 4 (2013): 273–79; and Mitchell L. Stevens, "Culture and Education," *Annals of the American Academy of Political and Social Science* 619, no. 1 (2008): 97–113. For critiques of quantitative approaches that document the intergenerational transmission of inequality but treat schools as "black boxes" in the process, see Bart Bonikowski, "Questioning Pedagogy: Reflections on the Critical Theory of the Curriculum," *The Discourse of Sociological Practice* 6 (2004): 41–50; and Annette Lareau, "Social Class Differences in Family-School Relationships: The Importance of Cultural Capital," *Sociology of Education* 60, no. 2

CONCLUSION

(1987): 73–85. For examples of studies that address this gap by drawing on ethnographic and other qualitative methods to unpack the processes *within* schools that contribute to inequality in outcomes, see Prudence L. Carter, *Keepin' It Real: School Success Beyond Black and White* (Oxford: Oxford University Press, 2005); Prudence L. Carter, *Stubborn Roots: Race, Culture, and Inequality in U.S. and South African Schools* (Oxford: Oxford University Press, 2012); Annette Lareau and Erin McNamara Horvat, "Moments of Social Inclusion and Exclusion: Race, Class, and Cultural Capital in Family-School Relationships," *Sociology of Education* 72, no. 1 (1999): 37–53; and Karolyn Tyson, *Integration Interrupted: Tracking, Black Students, and Acting White After Brown* (Oxford: Oxford University Press, 2011).

5. See Robert Dreeben, *On What Is Learned in School* (Boston: Addison Wesley, 1968), for a discussion of the importance of studying the nonacademic outcomes of schooling.

6. Beyond Glenville and Roxbridge, Sarah Godsell describes how preservice teachers in university classes engage with an earlier version of the argument presented in chapter 3 of this book. She documents how they often defend the "both sides of the story" approach that I describe (frequently attributing to it a sense of neutrality). See Sarah Godsell, "'Both Sides of the Story': The Epistemic Nature of Historical Knowledge as Understood by Pre-Service History Teachers in a South African University," in *Teachers and the Epistemology of History*, ed. H. Å Elmersjö and P. Zanazanian (Palgrave Macmillan, forthcoming); and Chana Teeger, "'Both Sides of the Story': History Education in Post-apartheid South Africa," *American Sociological Review* 80, no. 6 (2015): 1175–1200. Research conducted by Natasha Robinson in Cape Town also corroborates many of my findings—especially as they pertain to racially diverse schools—adding support to the idea that these dynamics are not limited to Glenville and Roxbridge. Similar to this study, Robinson also finds an avoidance of discussions of structural continuities and an emphasis on emotion (in the past people "hated" each other; to overcome racism, we should "treat each other kindly"). See Natasha Robinson, "History Education for Transitional Justice: How Students Understand and Construct Historical Legacies in the Post-Apartheid South African History Classroom" (PhD diss., University of Oxford, 2020); and Natasha Robinson, "Developing Historical Consciousness for Social Cohesion: How South African Students Learn to Construct the Relationship Between Past and Present," in *Historical*

CONCLUSION

Justice and History Education, ed. Matilda Keynes, Henrik Åström Elmersjö, Daniel Lindmark, Björn Norlin, (Cham, Switzerland: Palgrave, 2021) 341–63. See also Diefendorf and Pascoe's discussion of the "love discourse" found in white organizations: Sarah Diefendorf and C. J. Pascoe, "In the Name of Love: White Organizations and Racialized Emotions," *Social Problems* (2023). Different from this study, however, Robinson's research also includes a teacher in a school that enrolls only black African and Coloured students. This teacher did focus on historical continuities. Such findings point to the presence of other types of discourses that might predominate in schools where white students do not enroll. But see Dryden-Peterson and Robinson's study of Plain High in Mitchells Plain in Cape Town (an area designated as "Coloured" during apartheid). Sarah Dryden-Peterson and Natasha Robinson, "Time, Source, and Responsibility: Understanding Changing Uses of the Past in 'Post-Conflict' South African History Teaching, 1998 and 2019," *Compare: A Journal of Comparative and International Education* (2023): 1–19. The study compares two points in time at the same school: 1998 and 2019. In the first point in time, teachers highlighted structural continuities between past and present. In the second, they drew a boundary around the past and focused on tropes of individual responsibility. Taken together, these studies suggest that we pay more attention to teaching history in both monoracial and multiracial schools and attend to how teaching changes over time.

7. See chapter 3, note 18 for an elaboration of Swidler's view of culture as a "tool-kit": Ann Swidler, "Culture in Action: Symbols and Strategies," *American Sociological Review* 51, no. 2 (1986): 273. Swidler further distinguishes between "settled" and "unsettled" lives. In the latter, culture is expressed as ideology, while in the former it becomes tradition or common sense. The current study has demonstrated how ideologies of reconciliation articulated during the "unsettled" times of the transition to democracy have solidified into a type of common sense in the cultural tool-kit of individuals living in the relatively "settled" times of the contemporary era.

8. For further discussion of EFF policy statements, see Sithembile Mbete, "Out with the Old, in with the New? The ANC and EFF's Battle to Represent the South African 'People,'" in *Populism in Global Perspective*, ed. Pierre Ostiguy, Francisco Panizza, and Benjamin Moffitt, (New York: Routledge, 2020) 240–54.

CONCLUSION

9. See, for example, Sithembile Mbete, "The Economic Freedom Fighters: South Africa's Turn Towards Populism?," *Journal of African Elections* 14, no. 1 (2015): 35–59; Noor Nieftagodien, "The Economic Freedom Fighters and the Politics of Memory and Forgetting," *South Atlantic Quarterly* 114, no. 2 (2015): 446–56; and Benjamin Roberts, "Economic Freedom Fighters: Authoritarian or Democratic Contestant?," in *Election 2019: Change and Stability in South Africa's Democracy*, ed. Collette Schulz-Herzenberg and Roger Southall, (Johannesburg: Konrad-Adenauer Stiftung, 2019) 97–113.
10. On the racial coding of educational spaces, see Mark Hunter, *Race for Education: Gender, White Tone, and Schooling in South Africa* (Cambridge: Cambridge University Press, 2019); Simone Ispa-Landa and Jordan Conwell, "'Once You Go to a White School, You Kind of Adapt': Black Adolescents and the Racial Classification of Schools," *Sociology of Education* 88, no. 1 (2015): 1–19; and Rob Pattman and Ronelle Carolissen, eds., *Transforming Transformation in Research and Teaching at South African Universities* (Stellenbosch, South Africa: African Sun Media, 2018). For a broader discussion of racialized organizations (of which schools are a prime example), see Victor Ray, "A Theory of Racialized Organizations," *American Sociological Review* 84, no. 1 (2019): 26–53. On race, space, and the Rhodes Must Fall movement at UCT, see Shose Kessi, "The Fall of Rhodes: A Photovoice Investigation into Institutional Culture and Resistance at UCT," in *Transforming Transformation in Research and Teaching at South African Universities*, ed. Rob Pattman and Ronelle Carolissen, (Stellenbosch, South Africa: African Sun Media, 2018) 163–78; and Shose Kessi and Josephine Cornell, "Coming to UCT: Black Students, Transformation and Discourses of Race," *Journal of Student Affairs in Africa* 3, no. 2 (2015): 1–16. See also Susan Booysen, ed., *Fees Must Fall: Student Revolt, Decolonisation and Governance in South Africa* (Johannesburg: Wits University Press, 2016) for discussions of the links between the Rhodes Must Fall and Fees Must Fall movements; factors that distinguished the Fees Must Fall movement from prior fees protests in South African universities; and how students linked their struggle against fees with workers' struggles against outsourcing.
11. Harold Garfinkel, "Studies in Ethnomethodology," in *Social Theory Re-Wired*, ed. Wesley Longhofer and Daniel Winchester, (New York: Routledge, 2023) 58–66.

CONCLUSION

12. For an accessible overview of the intellectual origins, key concepts, and arguments of critical race theory, in particular how they connect to sociological questions, see Victor Ray, *On Critical Race Theory: Why It Matters and Why You Should Care* (New York: Random House, 2023).
13. See Ray, "*On Critical Race Theory.*" See also Prudence L. Carter, "Unrealized Integration in Education, Sociology, and Society," *American Sociological Review* 89, no. 1 (2024): 6–30. For a discussion of how political backlashes and reversals often follow in the wake of gains made by civil rights movements.
14. For discussions of the different forms that denial can take, see Stanley Cohen, *States of Denial: Knowing About Atrocities and Suffering* (New York: Wiley, 2013).
15. On the distinction between overt and covert silences, Vinitzky-Seroussi and Teeger argue that both can be deployed in the aim of enhancing memory or forgetting. See Vered Vinitzky-Seroussi and Chana Teeger, "Unpacking the Unspoken: Silence in Collective Memory and Forgetting," *Social Forces* 88, no. 3 (2010): 1103–22; and Vered Vinitzky-Seroussi and Chana Teeger, "Silence and Collective Memory," in *Oxford Handbook of Cognitive Sociology*, ed. Wayne H. Brekhus and Gabe Ignatow, (New York: Oxford University Press, 2019) 663–74. On silent, but embodied, forms of memory, see Carol A. Kidron, "Toward an Ethnography of Silence: The Lived Presence of the Past in the Everyday Life of Holocaust Trauma Survivors and Their Descendants in Israel," *Current Anthropology* 50, no. 1 (2009): 5–27. On the movement from silence to talk among survivors and their descendants, see Arlene Stein, *Reluctant Witnesses: Survivors, Their Children, and the Rise of Holocaust Consciousness* (Oxford: Oxford University Press, 2014). For a broad discussion of silence and denial in everyday life, see Eviatar Zerubavel, *The Elephant in the Room: Silence and Denial in Everyday Life* (Oxford: Oxford University Press, 2006). For discussions of denial among perpetrator groups, including the relationship between denial and stigma management, see Joachim J. Savelsberg, "Writing Biography in the Face of Cultural Trauma: Nazi Descent and the Management of Spoiled Identities," *American Journal of Cultural Sociology* 10, no. 1 (2022): 34–64; and Joachim J. Savelsberg, *Knowing About Genocide: Armenian Suffering and Epistemic Struggles* (Berkeley: University of California Press, 2021). For a discussion of silence as a form of international impression management, see Lauren A. Rivera,

METHODOLOGICAL APPENDIX

"Managing 'Spoiled' National Identity: War, Tourism, and Memory in Croatia," *American Sociological Review* 73, no. 4 (2008): 613–34.

16. For a discussion of this debate, see M. Noor Davids, "'Making History Compulsory': Politically Inspired or Pedagogically Justifiable?," *Yesterday and Today* no. 15 (2016): 84–102.

METHODOLOGICAL APPENDIX

1. Mario Luis Small, "'How Many Cases Do I Need?' On Science and the Logic of Case Selection in Field-Based Research," *Ethnography* 10, no. 1 (2009): 5–38; see also Robert K. Yin, *Case Study Research: Design and Methods*, 4th ed. (Thousand Oaks, CA: Sage, 2009).
2. For more information about the desegregation of South African schools, see Mark Hunter, *Race for Education: Gender, White Tone, and Schooling in South Africa* (Cambridge: Cambridge University Press, 2019); Crain Soudien, *Realising the Dream: Unlearning the Logic of Race in the South African School* (Cape Town: HSRC Press, 2012); and Chana Teeger, "Ruptures in the Rainbow Nation: How Desegregated South African Schools Deal with Interpersonal and Structural Racism," *Sociology of Education* 88, no. 3 (2015): 226–43.
3. See Nadine E. Dolby, *Constructing Race: Youth, Identity, and Popular Culture in South Africa* (Albany: SUNY Press, 2001); Soudien, *Realising the Dream*.
4. Graeme Bloch, *The Toxic Mix: What's Wrong with South Africa's Schools and How to Fix It* (Cape Town: Tafelberg, 2009), 148.
5. See Prudence L. Carter, *Stubborn Roots: Race, Culture, and Inequality in U.S. and South African Schools* (Oxford: Oxford University Press, 2012); Soudien, *Realising the Dream*; and Teeger, "Ruptures in the Rainbow Nation."
6. In contrast, consider Holocaust education in Germany. There, the challenges are different because descendants of victims are notably absent; see Alexandra Oeser, *When Will We Talk About Hitler? German Students and the Nazi Past* (New York: Berghahn, 2019). The challenges are also different in Northern Ireland where the school system is, for the most part, segregated along religious lines; see Keith C. Barton and Alan W. McCully, "History, Identity, and the School Curriculum in Northern Ireland: An Empirical Study of Secondary Students' Ideas and Perspectives," *Journal of Curriculum Studies* 37, no. 1 (2005): 85–116. Similarly,

METHODOLOGICAL APPENDIX

in the Balkans, Serbs, Bosniaks, and Croats learn history in ethnically homogenous education systems; see Tamara Trošt and Jovana M. Trbovc, "Identity Politics in History Textbooks in the Region of the Former Yugoslavia," in *The Visegrad Four and the Western Balkans: Framing Regional Identities*, ed. Adam B. Balazs and Christina Griessler, (Baden-Baden, Germany: Nomos, 2020) 197–230. This is true even in ethnically mixed areas of Bosnia and Herzegovina, where a policy of "two schools under one roof" means that children study in ethnically segregated classrooms and follow different curricula within the same school; see A. D. Tveit, D. L. Cameron, and V. B. Kovač, "'Two Schools Under One Roof' in Bosnia and Herzegovina: Exploring the Challenges of Group Identity and Deliberative Values Among Bosniak and Croat Students," *International Journal of Educational Research* 66 (2014): 103–12.

7. Townships were urban areas zoned for black South Africans during apartheid. They remain largely racially segregated in the new dispensation.
8. As discussed in chapter 1, in South Africa, school zones are determined according to whether parents or guardians reside *or* work in the area.
9. Carter, *Stubborn Roots*; Saloshna Vandeyar and Roy Killen, "Teacher-Student Interactions in Desegregated Classrooms in South Africa," *International Journal of Educational Development* 26, no. 4 (2006): 382–93.
10. As discussed in chapter 4, all South African students have to take at least two languages: one as a "first language" and another as a "second" or "additional" language.
11. Karl Mannheim, *Essays on the Sociology of Knowledge* (London: Routledge, 1952), 276–322; see also Howard Schuman and Jacqueline Scott, "Generations and Collective Memories," *American Sociological Review* 54, no. 3 (1989): 359–81.
12. Erik H. Erikson, *Identity: Youth and Crisis* (New York: Norton, 1968).
13. The South African school year runs from January until December. It is broken up into four terms with breaks in between. These breaks range from approximately three to four weeks each.
14. Life orientation (LO) is a subject that students are required to take up until Grade 12, although the mark that they receive on standardized tests for this subject does not influence their chances of going to university, where admission relies on explicit criteria based on matriculation results. LO covers a range of topics, including health and the environment, physical education, constitutional rights and responsibilities, self-development, and the world of work.

METHODOLOGICAL APPENDIX

15. I observed three additional classrooms very infrequently, due to scheduling conflicts between classes. These classes were taught by teachers whom I observed in other classrooms.
16. Johannesburg is in the province of Gauteng.
17. On racial categorization in South Africa, see Deborah Posel, "Race as Common Sense: Racial Classification in Twentieth-Century South Africa," *African Studies Review* 44, no. 2 (2001): 87–114.
18. As discussed in chapter 2, note 16, most students identified using one of apartheid's official racial categories, except for five students who identified as biracial or mixed.
19. I discuss the reasons for this in chapter 2.
20. Except, for example, when it came to understandings of the pass laws in the post-samples of the two schools, as discussed in chapter 4.
21. Nicole M. Deterding and Mary C. Waters, "Flexible Coding of In-Depth Interviews: A Twenty-First-Century Approach," *Sociological Methods and Research* 50, no. 2 (2018): 708–39.
22. Matthew B. Miles and A. Michael Huberman, *Qualitative Data Analysis: An Expanded Sourcebook* (Thousand Oaks, CA: Sage, 1994).
23. For discussions of reflexivity and positionality, see, for example, Lee Ann Fujii, *Interviewing in Social Science Research: A Relational Approach* (New York: Routledge, 2017); Kathleen Gerson and Sarah Damaske, *The Science and Art of Interviewing* (Oxford: Oxford University Press, 2020); and Marilys Guillemin and Lynn Gillam, "Ethics, Reflexivity, and 'Ethically Important Moments' in Research," *Qualitative Inquiry* 10, no. 2 (2004): 261–80.

BIBLIOGRAPHY

Anderson, Benedict. *Imagined Communities: Reflections on the Origin and Spread of Nationalism*. London: Verso, 2006.

Apple, Michael. *Ideology and Curriculum*. New York: Routledge, 2004.

Autry, Robyn. *Desgregating the Past: The Public Life of Memory in the United States and South Africa*. New York: Columbia University Press, 2017.

Banks, J. A. "Approaches to Multicultural Curriculum Reform." *Trotter Review* 3, no. 3 (1989): 17–19.

Barbalet, Jack M. "Boredom and Social Meaning." *British Journal of Sociology* 50, no. 4 (1999): 631–46.

Barton, Keith C., and Alan W. McCully. "History, Identity, and the School Curriculum in Northern Ireland: An Empirical Study of Secondary Students' Ideas and Perspectives." *Journal of Curriculum Studies* 37, no. 1 (2005): 85–116.

Bauman, Zygmunt. *Modernity and the Holocaust*. Ithaca, NY: Cornell University Press, 2000.

Bertram, Carol. "The Recontextualising Logics of Four Post-Colonial African School History Curriculum Documents: Kenya, Rwanda, South Africa and Zimbabwe." In *Teaching African History in Schools*, ed. Denise Bentrovato and Johan Wassermann, 15–44. Boston: Brill, 2021.

Bloch, Graeme. *The Toxic Mix: What's Wrong with South Africa's Schools and How to Fix It*. Cape Town: Tafelberg, 2009.

Blumer, Herbert. "Race Prejudice as a Sense of Group Position." *Pacific Sociological Review* 1, no. 1 (1958): 3–7.

BIBLIOGRAPHY

Bobo, Lawrence. "Race, Interests, and Beliefs About Affirmative Action: Unanswered Questions and New Directions." *American Behavioral Scientist* 41, no. 7 (1998): 985–1003.

Bobo, Lawrence, James R. Kluegel, and Ryan A. Smith. "Laissez-Faire Racism: The Crystallization of a Kinder, Gentler, Antiblack Ideology." In *Racial Attitudes in the 1990s: Continuity and Change*, ed. Steven A Tuch and Jack K. Martin, 15–42. Westport, CT: Praeger, 1997.

Boersema, Jacob R. *Can We Unlearn Racism? What South Africa Teaches Us About Whiteness*. Stanford, CA: Stanford University Press, 2022.

Bonikowski, Bart. "Questioning Pedagogy: Reflections on the Critical Theory of the Curriculum." *Discourse of Sociological Practice* 6 (2004): 41–50.

Bonilla-Silva, Eduardo. "Feeling Race: Theorizing the Racial Economy of Emotions." *American Sociological Review* 84, no. 1 (2019): 1–25.

———. "More than Prejudice: Restatement, Reflections, and New Directions in Critical Race Theory." *Sociology of Race and Ethnicity* 1, no. 1 (2015): 73–87.

———. *Racism Without Racists: Color-Blind Racism and the Persistence of Racial Inequality in America*. 6th ed. Lanham, MD: Rowman & Littlefield, 2021.

Bowles, Samuel, and Herbert Gintis. *Schooling in Capitalist America: Educational Reform and the Contradictions of Economic Life*. Chicago: Haymarket, 2011.

Booysen, Susan, ed. *Fees Must Fall: Student Revolt, Decolonisation and Governance in South Africa* Johannesburg: Wits University Press, 2016.

Brambilla, Marco, Marcella Ravenna, and Miles Hewstone. "Changing Stereotype Content Through Mental Imagery: Imagining Intergroup Contact Promotes Stereotype Change." *Group Processes and Intergroup Relations* 15, no. 3 (2012): 305–15.

Breidenstein, Georg. "The Meaning of Boredom in School Lessons. Participant Observation in the Seventh and Eighth Form." *Ethnography and Education* 2, no. 1 (2007): 93–108.

Brint, Steven. "The 'Collective Mind' at Work: A Decade in the Life of U.S. Sociology of Education." *Sociology of Education* 86, no. 4 (2013): 273–79.

Brissett, Dennis, and Robert P. Snow. "Boredom: Where the Future Isn't." *Symbolic Interaction* 16, no. 3 (1993): 237–56.

Brubaker, Rogers, and Frederick Cooper. "Beyond 'Identity.'" *Theory and Society* 29, no. 1 (2000): 1–47.

Brustein, William. *Roots of Hate: Anti-Semitism in Europe Before the Holocaust*. Cambridge: Cambridge University Press, 2003.

BIBLIOGRAPHY

Burawoy, Michael. "The Capitalist State in South Africa: Marxist and Sociological Perspectives on Race and Class." *Political Power and Social Theory* 2 (1981): 279–335.

Byrnes, Deborah A., and Gary Kiger. "Prejudice-Reduction Simulations: Ethics, Evaluations, and Theory into Practice." *Simulation and Gaming* 23, no. 4 (1992): 457–71.

Calarco, Jessica McCrory. "Coached for the Classroom: Parents' Cultural Transmission and Children's Reproduction of Educational Inequalities." *American Sociological Review* 79, no. 5 (2014): 1015–37.

Carr, Edward Hallett. *What Is History?* Hampshire: Palgrave, 2001.

Carter, Prudence L. *Keepin' It Real: School Success Beyond Black and White*. Oxford: Oxford University Press, 2005.

——. *Stubborn Roots: Race, Culture, and Inequality in U.S. and South African Schools*. Oxford: Oxford University Press, 2012.

——. "Unrealized Integration in Education, Sociology, and Society," *American Sociological Review* 89, no. 1 (2024): 6–30.

Chisholm, Linda. "The State of Curriculum Reform in South Africa: The Issue of Curriculum 2005." In *State of the Nation: South Africa 2003–2004*, ed. John Daniel, Adam Habib, and Roger Southall, 268–89. Cape Town: HSRC Press, 2003.

Cohen, Stanley. *States of Denial: Knowing About Atrocities and Suffering*. New York: Wiley, 2013.

Davids, M. Noor. "'Making History Compulsory': Politically Inspired or Pedagogically Justifiable?" *Yesterday and Today* no. 15 (2016): 84–102.

DeGloma, Thomas. "Awakenings: Autobiography, Memory, and the Social Logic of Personal Discovery." *Sociological Forum* 25, no. 3 (2010): 519–40.

——. *Seeing the Light: The Social Logic of Personal Discovery*. Chicago: University of Chicago Press, 2014.

Desmond, Matthew, and Mustafa Emirbayer. "What Is Racial Domination?" *Du Bois Review: Social Science Research on Race* 6, no. 2 (2009): 335–55.

Deterding, Nicole M., and Mary C. Waters. "Flexible Coding of In-Depth Interviews: A Twenty-First-Century Approach." *Sociological Methods and Research* 50, no. 2 (2018): 708–39.

Diefendorf, Sarah, and C. J. Pascoe. "In the Name of Love: White Organizations and Racialized Emotions." *Social Problems* (2023): spad019.

Doharty, Nadena. "The 'Angry Black Woman' as Intellectual Bondage: Being Strategically Emotional on the Academic Plantation." *Race Ethnicity and Education* 23, no. 4 (2020): 548–62.

BIBLIOGRAPHY

Dolby, Nadine E. *Constructing Race: Youth, Identity, and Popular Culture in South Africa*. Albany: SUNY Press, 2001.

Dooms, Tessa and Lynsey Ebony Chutel. *Coloured: How Classification Became Culture*. Johannesburg: Jonathan Ball, 2023.

Dreeben, Robert. *On What Is Learned in School*. Boston: Addison Wesley, 1968.

Dryden-Peterson, Sarah, and Natasha Robinson. "Time, Source, and Responsibility: Understanding Changing Uses of the Past in 'Post-Conflict' South African History Teaching, 1998 and 2019." *Compare: A Journal of Comparative and International Education* (2023): 1–19.

Duquette, Catherine. "Relating Historical Consciousness to Historical Thinking Through Assessment." In *New Directions in Assessing Historical Thinking*, ed. Kadriye Ercikan and Peter Seixas, 51–63. New York: Routledge, 2015.

Ellis, Stephen. "The Historical Significance of South Africa's Third Force." *Journal of Southern African Studies* 24, no. 2 (1998): 261–99.

Epstein, Terrie. *Interpreting National History: Race, Identity, and Pedagogy in Classrooms and Communities*. New York: Routledge, 2010.

Erasmus, Zimitri. *Coloured by History, Shaped by Place: New Perspectives on Coloured Identities in Cape Town*. Cape Town: Kwela, 2001.

Erikson, Erik H. *Identity: Youth and Crisis*. New York: Norton, 1968.

Evans, Richard J. *In Defence of History*. London: Granta, 2012.

Flores, David. "From Prowar Soldier to Antiwar Activist: Change and Continuity in the Narratives of Political Conversion Among Iraq War Veterans." *Symbolic Interaction* 39, no. 2 (2016): 196–212.

Fujii, Lee Ann. *Interviewing in Social Science Research: A Relational Approach*. New York: Routledge, 2017.

Galinsky, Adam D., and Gillian Ku. "The Effects of Perspective-Taking on Prejudice: The Moderating Role of Self-Evaluation." *Personality and Social Psychology Bulletin* 30, no. 5 (2004): 594–604.

Gardiner, Michael E. "Henri Lefebvre and the 'Sociology of Boredom.'" *Theory, Culture and Society* 29, no. 2 (2012): 37–62.

Garfinkel, Harold. "Studies in Ethnomethodology." In *Social Theory Re-Wired*, ed. Wesley Longhofer and Daniel Winchester, 58–66. New York: Routledge, 2023.

Gerson, Kathleen, and Sarah Damaske. *The Science and Art of Interviewing*. Oxford: Oxford University Press, 2020.

Gibson, James L. "Does Truth Lead to Reconciliation? Testing the Causal Assumptions of the South African Truth and Reconciliation Process." *American Journal of Political Science* 48, no. 2 (2004): 201–17.

BIBLIOGRAPHY

Godsell, Sarah. "'Both Sides of the Story': The Epistemic Nature of Historical Knowledge as Understood by Pre-Service History Teachers in a South African University." In *Teachers and the Epistemology of History*, ed. H. Å Elmersjö and P. Zanazanian (Palgrave Macmillan) (forthcoming).

Goldstone, Richard. "Forward." In *Looking Back, Reaching Forward: Reflections on the Truth and Reconciliation Commission of South Africa*, ed. Charles Villa-Vicencio and Wilhelm Verwoerd. Cape Town: University of Cape Town Press, 2000.

Guillemin, Marilys, and Lynn Gillam. "Ethics, Reflexivity, and 'Ethically Important Moments' in Research." *Qualitative Inquiry* 10, no. 2 (2004): 261–80.

Hagerman, Margaret A. *White Kids: Growing Up with Privilege in a Racially Divided America*. New York: New York University Press, 2018.

———. "White Families and Race: Colour-Blind and Colour-Conscious Approaches to White Racial Socialization." *Ethnic and Racial Studies* 37, no. 14 (2014): 2598–614.

Halberstadt, Amy G., Alison N. Cooke, Pamela W. Garner, Sherick A. Hughes, Dejah Oertwig, and Shevaun D. Neupert. "Racialized Emotion Recognition Accuracy and Anger Bias of Children's Faces." *Emotion* 22, no. 3 (2022): 403.

Hayner, Priscilla. "Same Species, Different Animal: How South Africa Compares to Truth Commissions Worldwide." In *Looking Back, Reaching Forward: Reflections on the Truth and Reconciliation Commission of South Africa*, ed. Charles Villa-Vicencio and Wilhelm Verwoerd, 32–41. Cape Town: University of Cape Town Press, 2000.

Hunter, Mark. *Race for Education: Gender, White Tone, and Schooling in South Africa*. Cambridge: Cambridge University Press, 2019.

Ispa-Landa, Simone, and Jordan Conwell. "'Once You Go to a White School, You Kind of Adapt': Black Adolescents and the Racial Classification of Schools." *Sociology of Education* 88, no. 1 (2015): 1–19.

Ispa-Landa, Simone, and Sara Thomas. "Race, Gender, and Emotion Work Among School Principals." *Gender and Society* 33, no. 3 (2019): 387–409.

Jansen, Jonathan D. *Knowledge in the Blood: Confronting Race and the Apartheid Past*. Stanford, CA: Stanford University Press, 2009

Jenkins, Richard. "Rethinking Ethnicity: Identity, Categorization and Power." *Ethnic and Racial Studies* 17, no. 2 (1994): 197–223.

Johnsen, Rasmus. "Boredom and Organization Studies." *Organization Studies* 37, no. 10 (2016): 1403–15.

BIBLIOGRAPHY

Kessi, S. "The Fall of Rhodes: A Photovoice Investigation into Institutional Culture and Resistance at UCT." In *Transforming Transformation in Research and Teaching at South African Universities*, ed. Rob Pattman and Ronelle Carolissen, 163–78. Stellenbosch, South Africa: African Sun Media, 2018.

Kessi, Shose, and Josephine Cornell. "Coming to UCT: Black Students, Transformation and Discourses of Race." *Journal of Student Affairs in Africa* 3, no. 2 (2015): 1–16.

Kidron, Carol A. "Toward an Ethnography of Silence: The Lived Presence of the Past in the Everyday Life of Holocaust Trauma Survivors and Their Descendants in Israel." *Current Anthropology* 50, no. 1 (2009): 5–27.

Kiguwa, Peace. "The Rainbow Nation: Constructs of National Identity in Post-Apartheid South Africa." In *A Race Against Time: Psychology and Challenges to Deracialisation in South Africa*, ed. Garth Stevens, Vijé Franchi, and Tanya Swart, 317–34. Pretoria: University of South Africa, 2006.

Kinder, Donald R., and David O. Sears. "Prejudice and Politics: Symbolic Racism Versus Racial Threats to the Good Life." *Journal of Personality and Social Psychology* 40, no. 3 (1981): 414.

Lamont, Michèle, and Virág Molnár. "The Study of Boundaries in the Social Sciences." *Annual Review of Sociology* 28, no. 1 (2002): 167–95.

Lareau, Annette. "Social Class Differences in Family-School Relationships: The Importance of Cultural Capital." *Sociology of Education* 60, no. 2 (1987): 73–85.

Lareau, Annette, and Erin McNamara Horvat. "Moments of Social Inclusion and Exclusion: Race, Class, and Cultural Capital in Family-School Relationships." *Sociology of Education* 72, no. 1 (1999): 37–53.

Lewis, Amanda E. *Race in the Schoolyard: Negotiating the Color Line in Classrooms and Communities*. New Brunswick, NJ: Rutgers University Press, 2003.

Lewis, Amanda E., and John B. Diamond. *Despite the Best Intentions: How Racial Inequality Thrives in Good Schools*. Oxford: Oxford University Press, 2015.

Lockhart, P. R. "Schools Keep Teaching Slavery and Civil Rights History in Ways That Traumatize Black Students." *Vox*, April 19, 2019.

Lodge, Tom. *Politics in South Africa: From Mandela to Mbeki*. Bloomington: Indiana University Press, 2003.

Loseke, Donileen R. "Examining Emotion as Discourse: Emotion Codes and Presidential Speeches Justifying War." *Sociological Quarterly* 50, no. 3 (2009): 497–524.

BIBLIOGRAPHY

Mamdani, Mahmood. "A Diminished Truth." *Siyaya!* 3 (1998): 38–41.
Mannheim, Karl. *Essays on the Sociology of Knowledge.* London: Routledge, 1952.
Marx, Anthony W. *Making Race and Nation: A Comparison of South Africa, the United States, and Brazil.* Cambridge: Cambridge University Press, 1998.
Mbete, Sithembile. "The Economic Freedom Fighters: South Africa's Turn Towards Populism?" *Journal of African Elections* 14, no. 1 (2015): 35–59.
———. "Out with the Old, in with the New? The ANC and EFF's Battle to Represent the South African 'People.'" In *Populism in Global Perspective*, ed. Pierre Ostiguy, Francisco Panizza, and Benjamin Moffitt, 240–54. New York: Routledge, 2020.
McGregor, Lorna. "Individual Accountability in South Africa: Cultural Optimum or Political Façade?" *American Journal of International Law* 95, no. 1 (2001): 32–45.
Miles, Matthew B., and A. Michael Huberman. *Qualitative Data Analysis: An Expanded Sourcebook.* Thousand Oaks, CA: Sage, 1994.
Mills, Charles. "White Ignorance." In *Race and Epistemologies of Ignorance*, eds. Shannon Sullivan and Nancy Tuana, 13–38, Albany: SUNY Press 2007, 13–38 247 (2007): 26–31.
Milner Jr., Murray. *Freaks, Geeks, and Cool Kids: American Teenagers, Schools, and the Culture of Consumption.* New York: Routledge, 2013.
Minow, Martha. "Between Vengeance and Forgiveness: South Africa's Truth and Reconciliation Commission." *Negotiation Journal* 14, no. 4 (1998): 319–55.
Mirchandani, Kiran. "Challenging Racial Silences in Studies of Emotion Work: Contributions from Anti-Racist Feminist Theory." *Organization Studies* 24, no. 5 (2003): 721–42.
Morris, Edward W. "'Tuck in That Shirt!' Race, Class, Gender, and Discipline in an Urban School." *Sociological Perspectives* 48, no. 1 (2005): 25–48.
Mueller, Jennifer C. "Racial Ideology or Racial Ignorance? An Alternative Theory of Racial Cognition." *Sociological Theory* 38, no. 2 (2020): 142–69.
Nelson, Jennifer L., and Tiffany D. Johnson. "How White Workers Navigate Racial Difference in the Workplace: Social-Emotional Processes and the Role of Workplace Racial Composition." *Work and Occupations* (2023). https://doi.org/10.07308884231176833.
Nieftagodien, Noor. "The Economic Freedom Fighters and the Politics of Memory and Forgetting." *South Atlantic Quarterly* 114, no. 2 (2015): 446–56.
Oeser, Alexandra. *When Will We Talk About Hitler? German Students and the Nazi Past.* New York: Berghahn, 2019.

Olick, Jeffrey K. "Collective Memory: The Two Cultures." *Sociological Theory* 17, no. 3 (1999): 333–48.

———. *In the House of the Hangman: The Agonies of German Defeat, 1943–1949.* Chicago: University of Chicago Press, 2005.

———. *The Politics of Regret: On Collective Memory and Historical Responsibility.* New York: Routledge, 2007.

Passerini, Luisa. *Fascism in Popular Memory: The Cultural Experience of the Turin Working Class.* Cambridge: Cambridge University Press, 1987.

Pattman, Rob, and Ronelle Carolissen, eds. *Transforming Transformation in Research and Teaching at South African Universities.* Stellenbosch, South Africa: African Sun Media, 2018.

Pérez, Raúl. *The Souls of White Jokes: How Racist Humor Fuels White Supremacy.* Stanford, CA: Stanford University Press, 2022.

Pirtle, Whitney N. Laster. "'White People Still Come Out on Top': The Persistence of White Supremacy in Shaping Coloured South Africans' Perceptions of Racial Hierarchy and Experiences of Racism in Post-Apartheid South Africa." *Social Sciences* 11, no. 2 (2022): 70.

Pollock, Mica. *Colormute: Race Talk Dilemmas in an American School.* Princeton, NJ: Princeton University Press, 2009.

Posel, Deborah. "Race as Common Sense: Racial Classification in Twentieth-Century South Africa." *African Studies Review* 44, no. 2 (2001): 87–114.

———. "The TRC Report: What Kind of History? What Kind of Truth?" In *Commissioning the Past: Understanding South Africa's Truth and Reconciliation Commission*, ed. Deborah Posel and Graeme Simpson, 147–72. Johannesburg: Witwatersrand University Press, 2002.

Quillian, Lincoln. "New Approaches to Understanding Racial Prejudice and Discrimination." *Annual Review of Sociology* 32 (2006): 299–328.

Ray, Victor. *On Critical Race Theory: Why It Matters and Why You Should Care.* New York: Random House, 2023.

———. "A Theory of Racialized Organizations." *American Sociological Review* 84, no. 1 (2019): 26–53.

Reyes, Victoria. "Ethnographic Toolkit: Strategic Positionality and Researchers' Visible and Invisible Tools in Field Research." *Ethnography* 21, no. 2 (2020): 220–40.

Rivera, Lauren A. "Managing 'Spoiled' National Identity: War, Tourism, and Memory in Croatia." *American Sociological Review* 73, no. 4 (2008): 613–34.

Roberts, Benjamin. "Economic Freedom Fighters: Authoritarian or Democratic Contestant?" In *Election 2019: Change and Stability in South Africa's*

BIBLIOGRAPHY

Democracy, ed. Collette Schulz-Herzenberg and Roger Southall, 97–113. Johannesburg: Konrad-Adenauer Stiftung, 2019.

Robinson, Natasha. "Conceptualising Historical Legacies for Transitional Justice History Education in Postcolonial Societies." *History Education Research Journal* 19, no. 1 (2022): 1–15.

——. "Developing Historical Consciousness for Social Cohesion: How South African Students Learn to Construct the Relationship Between Past and Present." In *Historical Justice and History Education*, ed. Matilda Keynes, Henrik Åström Elmersjö, Daniel Lindmark, Björn Norlin, 341–63. Cham, Switzerland: Palgrave, 2021.

——. "History Education for Transitional Justice: How Students Understand and Construct Historical Legacies in the Post-Apartheid South African History Classroom." PhD diss., University of Oxford, 2020.

——. "Using Holocaust Education as a 'Bridge' to Learning about Apartheid in a South African History Classroom: The Development of 'Interpretive frames' through Comparative Histories." *Holocaust and Genocide Studies* (forthcoming).

Robinson, Natasha, and Nicholas Kerswill. "'Myth' or 'Construct'?: What Students are Learning about Race in the South African History Classroom." *Yesterday and Today* 29, no. 1 (2023): 52–71.

Savelsberg, Joachim J. *Knowing About Genocide: Armenian Suffering and Epistemic Struggles*. Berkeley: University of California Press, 2021.

——. "Writing Biography in the Face of Cultural Trauma: Nazi Descent and the Management of Spoiled Identities." *American Journal of Cultural Sociology* 10, no. 1 (2022): 34–64.

Schrock, Douglas, Janice McCabe, and Christian Vaccaro. "Narrative Manhood Acts: Batterer Intervention Program Graduates' Tragic Relationships." *Symbolic Interaction* 41, no. 3 (2018): 384–410.

Schuman, Howard, and Cheryl Rieger. "Historical Analogies, Generational Effects, and Attitudes Toward War." *American Sociological Review* 57, no. 3 (1992): 315–26.

Schuman, Howard, and Jacqueline Scott. "Generations and Collective Memories." *American Sociological Review* 54, no. 3 (1989): 359–81.

Schuman, Howard, Vered Vinitzky-Seroussi, and Amiram D. Vinokur. "Keeping the Past Alive: Memories of Israeli Jews at the Turn of the Millennium." *Sociological Forum* 18, no. 1 (2003): 103–36.

Sears, David O. "Symbolic Racism." In *Eliminating Racism: Profiles in Controversy*, ed. Phyllis A. Katz and Dalmas A. Taylor, 53–84. New York: Springer, 1988.

BIBLIOGRAPHY

Seekings, Jeremy, and Nicoli Nattrass. *Class, Race, and Inequality in South Africa*. New Haven, CT: Yale University Press, 2008.

Seixas, Peter. "A Model of Historical Thinking." *Educational Philosophy and Theory* 49, no. 6 (2017): 593–605.

Simko, Christina. *The Politics of Consolation: Memory and the Meaning of September 11*. Oxford: Oxford University Press, 2015.

Simpson, Graeme. "Tell No Lies, Claim No Easy Victories: A Brief Evaluation of South Africa's Truth and Reconciliation Commission." In *Commissioning the Past: Understanding South Africa's Truth and Reconciliation Commission*, ed. Deborah Posel and Graeme Simpson, 220–51. Johannesburg: Witwatersrand University Press, 2002.

Small, Mario Luis. "'How Many Cases Do I Need?' On Science and the Logic of Case Selection in Field-Based Research." *Ethnography* 10, no. 1 (2009): 5–38.

Soudien, Crain. *Realising the Dream: Unlearning the Logic of Race in the South African School*. Cape Town: HSRC Press, 2012.

Stein, Arlene. *Reluctant Witnesses: Survivors, Their Children, and the Rise of Holocaust Consciousness*. Oxford: Oxford University Press, 2014.

Stephens, Nicole M., Lauren A. Rivera, and S. Townsend. "What Works to Increase Diversity? A Multi-Level Approach." *Research in Organizational Behavior* 39 (2020): 1–51.

Stevens, Mitchell L. "Culture and Education." *Annals of the American Academy of Political and Social Science* 619, no. 1 (2008): 97–113.

Steyn, Melissa. "The Ignorance Contract: Recollections of Apartheid Childhoods and the Construction of Epistemologies of Ignorance." *Identities* 19, no. 1 (2012): 8–25.

Stryker, Sheldon, and Peter J. Burke. "The Past, Present, and Future of an Identity Theory." *Social Psychology Quarterly* 63, no. 4 (2000): 284–97.

Swidler, Ann. "Culture in Action: Symbols and Strategies." *American Sociological Review* 51, no. 2 (1986): 273–86.

Teeger, Chana. "Collective Memory and Collective Fear: How South Africans Use the Past to Explain Crime." *Qualitative Sociology* 37, no. 1 (2014): 69–92.

———. "'Both Sides of the Story': History Education in Post-apartheid South Africa." *American Sociological Review* 80, no. 6 (2015): 1175–1200.

———. "(Not) Feeling the Past: Boredom as a Racialized Emotion." *American Journal of Sociology* 129, no. 1 (2023): 1–40.

———. "Ruptures in the Rainbow Nation: How Desegregated South African Schools Deal with Interpersonal and Structural Racism." *Sociology of Education* 88, no. 3 (2015): 226–43.

BIBLIOGRAPHY

Teeger, Chana, and Vered Vinitzky-Seroussi. "Controlling for Consensus: Commemorating Apartheid in South Africa." *Symbolic Interaction* 30, no. 1 (2007): 57–78.

Tochilnikova, Elina. *Towards a General Theory of Boredom: A Case Study of Anglo and Russian Society*. New York: Routledge, 2020.

Trošt, Tamara. "History Textbooks and Transitional Justice." In *The Oxford Handbook of Transitional Justice*, ed. Jens Meierhenrich, Alexander Laban Hinton, and Lawrence Douglas. New York: Oxford University Press, 2023.

——— "Ruptures and Continuities in Nationhood Narratives: Reconstructing the Nation Through History Textbooks in Serbia and Croatia." *Nations and Nationalism* 24, no. 3 (2018): 716–40.

Trošt, Tamara P., and Jovana M. Trbovc. "Identity Politics in History Textbooks in the Region of the Former Yugoslavia." In *The Visegrad Four and the Western Balkans: Framing Regional Identities*, ed. Adam B. Balazs and Christina Griessler, 197–230. Baden-Baden: Nomos, 2020.

Tveit, A. D., D. L. Cameron, and V. B. Kovač. "'Two Schools Under One Roof' in Bosnia and Herzegovina: Exploring the Challenges of Group Identity and Deliberative Values Among Bosniak and Croat Students." *International Journal of Educational Research* 66 (2014): 103–12.

Tyson, Karolyn. *Integration Interrupted: Tracking, Black Students, and Acting White After Brown*. Oxford: Oxford University Press, 2011.

Vandeyar, Saloshna and Roy Killen. "Teacher–Student Interactions in Desegregated Classrooms in South Africa." *International Journal of Educational Development* 26, no. 4 (2006): 382–93.

Vinitzky-Seroussi, Vered. "Commemorating a Difficult Past: Yitzhak Rabin's Memorials." *American Sociological Review* 67, no. 1 (2002): 30–51.

———. *Yitzhak Rabin's Assassination and the Dilemmas of Commemoration*. Albany, NY: State University of New York Press, 2010.

Vinitzky-Seroussi, Vered, and Chana Teeger. "Silence and Collective Memory." In *Oxford Handbook of Cognitive Sociology*, ed. Wayne H. Brekhus and Gabe Ignatow, 663–74. New York: Oxford University Press, 2019.

———. "Unpacking the Unspoken: Silence in Collective Memory and Forgetting." *Social Forces* 88, no. 3 (2010): 1103–22.

Wagner-Pacifici, Robin. "Theorizing the Restlessness of Events." *American Journal of Sociology* 115, no. 5 (2010): 1351–86.

Warikoo, Natasha. "Addressing Emotional Health While Protecting Status: Asian American and White Parents in Suburban America." *American Journal of Sociology* 126, no. 3 (2020): 545–76.

BIBLIOGRAPHY

Waters, Mary C. *Black Identities: West Indian Immigrant Dreams and American Realities.* Cambridge, MA: Harvard University Press, 1999.

Weiner, Melissa F. "(E)RACING SLAVERY: Racial Neoliberalism, Social Forgetting, and Scientific Colonialism in Dutch Primary School History Textbooks." *Du Bois Review: Social Science Research on Race* 11, no. 2 (2014): 329–51.

Weldon, Gail. "Memory, Identity and the Politics of Curriculum Construction in Transition Societies: Rwanda and South Africa." *Perspectives in Education* 27, no. 2 (2009): 177–89.

Whitehead, Kevin A. "'Categorizing the Categorizer': The Management of Racial Common Sense in Interaction." *Social Psychology Quarterly* 72, no. 4 (2009): 325-342.

Wilkins, Amy C., and Jennifer A. Pace. "Class, Race, and Emotions." In *Handbook of the Sociology of Emotions: Volume II*, ed. Jan E. Stets and Jonathan H. Turner, 385–409. New York: Springer, 2014.

Willis, John S. "Who Needs Multicultural Education? White Students, U.S. History, and the Construction of a Usable Past." *Anthropology and Education Quarterly* 27, no. 3 (1996): 365-89.

Wilson, Richard A. *The Politics of Truth and Reconciliation in South Africa: Legitimizing the Post-Apartheid State.* Cambridge: Cambridge University Press, 2001.

Wingfield, Adia Harvey. "Are Some Emotions Marked 'Whites Only'? Racialized Feeling Rules in Professional Workplaces." *Social Problems* 57, no. 2 (2010): 251–68.

———. "The Modern Mammy and the Angry Black Man: African American Professionals' Experiences with Gendered Racism in the Workplace." *Race, Gender and Class* 14, no. 1/2 (2007): 196–212.

Wolpe, Harold. "Capitalism and Cheap Labour-Power in South Africa: From Segregation to Apartheid." *Economy and Society* 1, no. 4 (1972): 425–56.

Yazdiha, Hajar. *The Struggle for the People's King.* Princeton, NJ: Princeton University Press, 2023.

Yin, Robert K. *Case Study Research: Design and Methods.* 4th ed. Thousand Oaks, CA: Sage, 2009.

Zagacki, Kenneth S. "Rhetoric, Dialogue, and Performance in Nelson Mandela's 'Televised Address on the Assassination of Chris Hani.'" *Rhetoric and Public Affairs* 6, no. 4 (2003): 709–35.

Zembylas, Michalinos. "'Pedagogy of Discomfort' and Its Ethical Implications: The Tensions of Ethical Violence in Social Justice Education." *Ethics and Education* 10, no. 2 (2015): 163–74.

BIBLIOGRAPHY

Zerubavel, Eviatar. *The Elephant in the Room: Silence and Denial in Everyday Life*. Oxford: Oxford University Press, 2006.

———. "In the Beginning: Notes on the Social Construction of Historical Discontinuity." *Sociological Inquiry* 63, no. 4 (1993): 457–59.

Zolberg, Vera L. "Museums as Contested Sites of Remembrance: The Enola Gay Affair." *Sociological Review* 43, no. S1 (1995): 69–82.

INDEX

Page numbers in *italics* indicate figures or tables.

academic outcomes, 128–29
activism, 172n7
affirmative action, 20–21, 110. *See also* black economic empowerment (BEE)
African National Congress (ANC): education and, 26; Freedom Charter, 175n1; IFP and, 159; Malema and, 131; PAC and, 52–53, 166n15; politics of, 123, 159n14; Youth League, 96–97
"Afrikaans classes," 70–71, 74–75, 79, 146. *See also* simulations
amnesty, 159n18
ANC. *See* African National Congress
ANC Youth League, 96–97
Anderson, Benedict, 9
anger, 66, 113

apartheid: anti-apartheid activism, 172n7; Apartheid Museum, 148–49; black Africans and, 1–2, 88, 125; consequences of, 115–24, *117*; Glenville High School during, 144–45; in history education, 59–60, 63, 71–72, 101–2, 129–35; history of, 73–74; Holocaust and, 24, 30–36, 153; language in, 171n1; legacy of, 112–15, *114*; National Party and, 47; oppression in, 49–50; and PAC, 53–55; Pass Laws, 89–90; racial hierarchies in, 74–75, 157n2, 158n7, 181n18; in RNCS, 26, 42; Roxbridge High School during, 144–45; segregation and, 50–51, 158n9; simulations of, 74–75, 79–84; in South Africa, 1–6, 25–27,

INDEX

apartheid (*continued*)
    27–28, 29–30, 58–59, 68; students
    and, 39–40, 51–52, *52*, 86–87,
    107–11, *108*; teachers of, 34–35, 105;
    TRC and, 19–20, 55–56; white
    South Africans during, 44–46,
    169n6; student interest in 20–21,
    25, 36–37
Asmal, Kader, 26–27
assassinations, 159n14, 173n16
authority: classroom dynamics and, 130;
    in education, 14–15; in simulations,
    81–82; teachers and, 17–18

Balkans, *28*, 29, 180n6
Banks, James A., 13
BEE policies. *See* Black Economic
    Empowerment policies
behavioral issues, 96
beneficiaries, 8, 47, 48, 64, 66, 121;
    victims and, 19
biracial: scholarship on, 166n16;
    students, 37, 56, 89, 104, *150*
black perpetrators, 47, 52–59
black Africans: apartheid and,
    1–2, 88, 125; desegregation for,
    3–4; at Glenville High School,
    41–42; Indians and, 113, 126–27;
    inequality for, 4–5; racial jokes
    and, 77–78; racism against, 67–68;
    at Roxbridge High School, 119;
    in South Africa, 166n18, 181n7; as
    students, 19–20, 36–37, 44–46, 111,
    115, 144–45, *145*, 154–55; teachers
    and, 6; violence and, 7; white
    South Africans and, 2–3, 14–15,
    39, 51–52, *52*, 82–83, 176n6; in Zulu
    classes, 70–71, 74, 122

Black Economic Empowerment
    (BEE) policies, 2, 4, 119
Black Lives Matter movement, 134
blanket amnesty, 159n18
Bobo, Lawrence, 116
Bonilla-Silva, Eduardo, 4–6
boredom, 19, 42, 168n22
"born frees," 1, 3, 107
both sides of the story. See equivalences

CAPS. *See* Curriculum and
    Assessment Policy Statement
Carter, Prudence L., 12
case selection, 143–47, *145*
categorization, 172n4
characteristics: of students, *150*,
    150–51; of teachers, *145*, 145–46
civil liberties, 10, 115–16
civil rights movement, 5, 27–28, 29
classroom dynamics: authority
    and, 130; discomfort in, 170n11;
    psychology of, 64–67; race and,
    44–46, 105–6; teachers and,
    120–21, 133–34; in Zulu class,
    94–96, 111
Cold War, *28*, 29
collective memory, 18, 163n47. *See also*
    memory
colonialism, 131–32
color-blindness, 134, 170n12
color-blind racial ideologies, 4–6
colormute racism, 11–12
Coloured: scholarship on, 166n15;
    students, 37, 39, 41, 50, 51, *52*, 74;
    township, 51
conflict, 13, 19, *28*, 44–46, 133;
    minimizing, 66,103; racialized, 103
Congress Alliance, 175n1

INDEX

consequences: apartheid and, 115–24, *117*; contemporary social problems as, 107–11, *108*; of education, 18; of history education, 18–19, 125; of interpersonal racism, 112–15, *114*
Constitution Hill, 148–49
contemporary social problems, 107–11, *108*
covert silence, 179n15
critical race theory, 134, 178n12
"cultural toolkit," 66
culture, 159, 177n7
Curriculum and Assessment Policy Statement (CAPS), 43, 147–48, 165n11
curriculum developers, 29–30
curriculum reform, 42–43

data analysis, 153–54
data collection: in-depth interviews, 149–52, *150*; observations, 148–49; written materials, 147–48
decolonization, 131–33
Defiance Campaign, 90–91, 166n15
democracy, 1–4, 6, 7, 13, 60
denial, 128, 134–35, 179nn14–15
desegregation, 3–4, 12, 16, 125, 162n35
discrimination, 85–86, 118, 121–22
District 9 (film), 39
diversity, 7, 126–27, 176n6; unity in, 1
de klerk, F. W. de, 7

Economic Freedom Fighters (EFF): history of, 97, 118; Malema and, 173n13; politics of, 161n26; reputation of, 130–31
economic inequality, 2, 5, 73–74

education: academic outcomes, 128–29; authority in, 14–15; collective memory in, 163n47; critical race theory in, 134; desegregation in, 125, 162n35; fieldwork in, 151–52; Freedom Charter in, 126–27; Gauteng Department of Education, 149; gender in, 92; at Glenville High School, 87–88; higher, 131–32, 147–48; Holocaust, 180n6; of Indian students, 104; Industrialization in, 37–38; juxtapositions in, 18–19; language, 146; Ministry of Basic Education, 27–28; Model-C schools, 143–46; national curriculum, 19; OBE, 26; race and, 69–70, 149–50; racial coding in, 178n10; at Roxbridge High School, 31–32; scholarship on, 175n4; segregation in, 20, 33–34; in South Africa, 108–9, 181n13; transition in, 127–28; TRC and, *28*; of white Africans, 19–20. *See also* history education
EFF. *See* Economic Freedom Fighters
Elliott, Jane, 173n16
empathy, 172n10
emotions, 47, 66, 122, 133, 167n21; anger, 66, 113; boredom, 19, 42, 168n22; fear, 44, 123; guilt, 6, 19, 59, 62–63, 66–67, 133; resentment, 116
Epstein, Terrie, 13
equal opportunity, 5, 124
equivalences: to black perpetrators, 52–59; in history education, 44–47, 64–68; juxtapositions and,

INDEX

equivalences (*continued*)
68; moral equivalence, 55–56; to whites, 47–52, *52*
excuses, 115–24, *117*
experiential learning, 20

fear, 44, 123
Fees Must Fall movement, 131, 178n10
formal observations, 148–49
Freedom Charter, 126–27, 166n15, 175n1

Gauteng Department of Education, 149
gender: National Women's Day, 80; National Women's March, 92; and the pass system, 72; race and, 90; sports and, 170n13; of teachers, 101–2; of whites, 98–99
Germany, 29, 30–31, 180n6. *See also* Holocaust
Glenville High School: academic performance at, 144; black Africans at, 41–42; diversity at, 176n6; education at, 87–88; enrollment at, 16–17; experiential learning at, 20; fieldwork at, 64, 96, 97, 151; history education at, 85–86, 98; poverty to, 157n4; race at, 109–10, 113, 144–45, *145*; Roxbridge High School and, 15–16, 30–34, 43, 64, 66–67, 69–70, 103–6, 126–29; simulations at, 70–71; students at, 58–59, 93, 119; teachers at, 22–25, 36, 44–48, 153–54; TRC lessons, 56–57; upward mobility at, 132; whites at, 71–72, 115–17. *See also specific topics*

Godsell, Sarah, 176n6
Government of National Unity, 6–7
grudges, 115–24, *117*
guilt, 6, 19, 59, 62–63, 66–67, 133

Hani, Chris, 159n14
hidden curriculum, 11, 15
hierarchies of interest, 30, 36–38
higher education, 131–32, 147–48
historical truncation of apartheid, 19, 43
history education: apartheid in, 59–60, 63, 71–72, 101–2, 129–35; cases from, 143–47, *145*; consequences of, 18–19, 125; contemporary social problems in, 107–11, *108*; data analysis of, 153–54; denial of, 134–35; disputes in, 133–34; equivalences in, 44–47, 64–68; in Germany, 180n6; at Glenville High School, 85–86, 98; hidden curriculum in, 11; historical consciousness in, 167n20; in in-depth interviews, 149–52, *150*; institutionalizing memory and, 6–10; juxtapositions in, 22–25, 30–36, 42–43; Mandela in, 58–59, 64–65; OBE in, 26; observations from, 148–49; positionality and, 154–55; production of, 17; psychology and, 146–47; race in, 1–6, 11–15, 47–52, *52*, 86–87, 112–15, *114*; research on, 176n6; in RNCS, 27, 29; at Roxbridge High School, 92–93, 96–98; scholarship on, 18–21, 165n9; segregation in, 93–94; simulations in, 69–70, 103–6; social science and, 173n12; in South Africa, 15–18, 37–38, 83,

INDEX

126–29; for students, 59–63; TRC in, 10, 64, 149; violence in, 56–57; why questions in, 38–42; written materials from, 147–48. *See also specific topics*
Hitler, Adolf, 25, 30–32, 41–42
Holocaust: apartheid and, 24, 30–36, 153; education, 180n6; human rights and, 165n10; juxtapositions with, 165n11; in RNCS, 23; for teachers, 24–25; World War II and, 29, 151
human rights, 27–28, 35–36, 165n10

identity: identification, 172n4; racial, 149–50, *150*, 166n16, 170n17; scholarship on, 163n43; of students, 119–20, 181n18; in youth, 13
ideology, 177n7
IFP. *See* Inkatha Freedom Party
in-depth interviews, 149–52, *150*
Indians: black Africans and, 113, 126–27; as students, 87–88, 104, 144–45, *145*
individualism, 62
Industrialization, 37–38
inequality: BEE and, 2; for black Africans, 4–5; in era of civil liberties, 10; in democracy, 3–4; economic, 73–74; equal opportunity and, 124; in hidden curriculum, 15; intraracial, 158n6; lessons on, 128–29; poverty and, 110; with resource allocation, 161n34; in socialization, 5–6; in South Africa, 11–15; structural, 133; to students, 105–6; talking about, 12; in TRC, 9–10; racialized, 3–5, 15, 46, 67, 89, 107–111, 120–125, 130–133
Inkatha Freedom Party (IFP), 159
institutionalizing memory, 6–10
interpersonal racism, 112–15, *114*
inter-racial trust, 160n25

Joseph, Helen, 79, 81, 172n7
juxtapositions: in education, 18–19; equivalences and, 68; with hierarchies of interest, 36–38; in history education, 22–25, 30–36, 42–43; in national curriculum, 25–27, 165n11, *27–28*, 29–30; in U.S. memory 169n8; for students, 38–42

King, Martin Luther, Jr., 169n8, 173n16
Kluegel, James R., 116
knowledge focus, *27–28*

Lamont, Michèle, 163n42
language: in apartheid, 171n1; culture and, 159; education, 146; isiXhosa, 159n18; isiZulu, 159n18; official, 127; pejorative, 76–77; race and, 70–71, 166n16, 171n1; in South Africa, 74–75, 173n15
legalized racism, 13–14
Lewis, Amanda E., 11–12
life orientation (LO), 148, 181n14
loyalty, 82–83

Malcolm X, 169n8
Malema, Julius, 96–97, 118, 131, 173n13
Mandela, Nelson: Chris Hani and 159n14; de Klerk and, 7; for Government of National Unity,

■ 201 ■

INDEX

Mandela (continued)
  6–7; in history education, 58–59, 64–65; TRC and, 10; trial of, 55
Mannheim, Karl, 146–47
Maxwele, Chumani, 131
Mbeki, Thabo, 159n14
melodrama, 165n12
memory, 6–10, 18. *See also* collective memory
micro-interactional problems, 66–67
Ministry of Basic Education, 27–28
MK. *See* Umkhonto we Sizwe
Model-C schools, 143–46. *See also* school desegregation
Molnár, Virág, 163n42
moral equivalence, 55–56
Motlanthe, Kgalema, 171n3

national curriculum, 19, 23, 25–27, *27–28*, 29–30
National Party, 34, 43, 47, 123
National Women's Day, 80
nation-building narratives, 160n24
Naudé, Beyers, 83
Nazis, 24, *27–28*, 31–32
Northern Ireland, 180n6
Nuclear Age, *28*, 29

OBE. *See* outcomes-based education
observations, 148–49, 181n15
Olick, Jeffrey, 163n47
outcomes-based education (OBE), 26
overt silence, 179n15

Pan African Congress (PAC), 52–55, 166n15
Pass Laws Act, 89–90, 172n11

politics: of ANC, 123, 159n14; of BEE, 4; of decolonization, 131–33; of EFF, 161n26; of loyalty, 82–83; of National Party, 34, 43, 47, 123; political backlashes, 178n13; political parties, 10; public discourse and, 130–31; of RDP, 170nn15–16; of reconciliation, 6–7; in South Africa, 52–55, 119–21; violence in, 159n15; of whites, 9
positionality, 154–55, 182n23
poverty, 4, 64, 95, 108–10, 157n4
private property rights, 159n17
production, of history education, 17
psychology: child development and, 146–47; of classroom dynamics, 64–67; denial, 134–35, 179n15; empathy, 172n10; melodrama, 165n12; of *ubuntu*, 7, 48, 148–49, 158n13, 169n3
public discourse, 130–31

race: classroom dynamics and, 44–46, 105–6; color-blindness, 4, 5, 14–15, 120, 134, 170n12; colormute racism, 11–12; discrimination by, 85–86; diversity of, 126–27; education and, 69–70, 149–50; gender and, 90; at Glenville High School, 109–10, 113, 144–45, *145*; in history education, 1–6, 11–15, 47–52, *52*, 86–87, 112–15, *114*; inter-racial trust, 160n25; intraracial inequality, 158n6; language and, 70–71, 166n16, 171n1; legalized racism, 5, 13–14, 155; race-conscious policies, 4; Racial Classification Board, 174n19; racial coding, 178n10;

INDEX

racial conflict, 13, 44–46, 103; racial hierarchies, 74–75, 157n2, 158n7, 181n18; racial identity, 149–50, *150*, 166n16, 170n17; racialized emotions, 167n21; racialized subjects, 104–5; racial jokes, 77–78; racism, 5, 11–14, 67–68, 98–102, 112–15, *114*, 115–16, 128–29, 152, 169n2; racism accusations, 101–2; racist laws, 24; resistance and, 80–81; reverse racism, 5; at Roxbridge High School, 71–72, 144–45, *145*; in simulations, 75–79, 93–100; social construction of, 103–6; social problems and, 108, *108*; in South Africa, 18–21; structural racism, 128; students' views on, 1–2, 51–52, 59–60 79–80, 87–89, *117*, 117–18, 119–124; symbolic racism, 115–16; teachers and, 100–101, 168n1, 171n2; in U.S., 20, 86 115–116, , 134, 169n8, 170n12, 173n16
racial categories in South Africa, 157n2
racialized emotions, 167n21
RDP. *See* Reconstruction and Development Programme
reconciliation, 6–8. *See also* Truth and Reconciliation Commission
Reconstruction and Development Programme (RDP), 64, 170nn15–16
resentment, 116
resistance: Defiance Campaign, 90–91; organizations, 8–9; race and, 80–81; to teachers, 81–82; violence in, 84

resource allocation, 123–24, 161n34
revenge, 115–24, *117*, 131
reverse racism, 5
"reverse apartheid" 53–54
Revised National Curriculum Statement (RNCS): apartheid in, 26, 37–38, 42; Asmal on, 26–27; CAPS and, 43, 147–48; curriculum developers and, 29–30; history education in, 27, 29; history of, 23; social sciences in, 173n12
Rhodes, Cecil John, 131
Rhodes Must Fall movement, 131, 178n10
RNCS. *See* Revised National Curriculum Statement
Robinson, Natasha, 176n6
role-playing, 102–3
Roxbridge High School: during apartheid, 144–45; black Africans at, 119; curriculum at, 23; data analysis and, 154; diversity at, 176n6; education at, 31–32; Glenville High School and, 15–16, 30–34, 43, 64, 66–67, 69–70, 103–6, 126–29; history education at, 92–93, 96–98; human rights at, 35–36; academic performance at, 144; race at, 71–72, 144–45, *145*; diversity at, 16–17; simulations and, 100–103; students at, 22–24, 40–41, 118; teachers at, 39–40, 48–50; upward mobility at, 132; visits to, 151; whites at, 62–63. *See also specific topics*

scholarship: on color-blind racial ideologies, 5–6; on culture, 177n7; on data analysis, 153–54;

INDEX

scholarship (*continued*)
on denial, 179n15; on education, 175n4; on history education, 18–21, 165n9; from history education cases, 143–47, *145*; on identity, 163n43; in-depth interviews in, 149–52, *150*; on nation-building narratives, 160n24; on positionality, 154–55; psychology and, 146–47; qualitative research, 154–55; on race, 4–5, 10–14, 115–116; on TRC, 8–9; on white supremacy, 169n4
Schuman, Howard, 58
Sears, David, 115–16
segregation: apartheid and, 50–51, 158n9; desegregation, 3–4, 12, 16, 125, 162n35; in education, 20, 33–34; in history education, 93–94; learning about, 88–89; structural violence of, 8
settler colonialism, 19. *See also* colonialism
Sharpeville Massacre, 166n15
silence, 13, 38, 61, 129, 179n15
simulations: of apartheid, 74–75, 79–84; at Glenville High School, 70–71; in history education, 69–70, 103–6; race in, 75–79, 93–100; to Roxbridge High School, 100–103; students and, 87–93; for teachers, 85–87; whites in, 71–74. *See also* role-playing
Small, Mario Luis, 143
Smith, Ryan A., 116
socialization, 5–6, 103–6
social justice, 172n7
social problems, 108, *108*

social sciences, 173n12
South Africa: apartheid in, 1–6, 25–27, *27–28*, 29–30, 58–59, 68; black Africans in, 166n18, 181n7; blanket amnesty in, 159n18; "born frees" in, 107; Britain and, 39; curriculum reform in, 42–43; decolonization in, 131–32; Defiance Campaign in, 90–91; education in, 108–9, 181n13; Freedom Charter in, 126–27; government of, 16; history education in, 15–18, 37–38, 83, 126–29; history of, 158n9, 171n3; Indian students in, 87–88; inequality in, 11–15; language in, 74–75, 173n15; Ministry of Basic Education in, 27–28; Model-C schools in, 143–46; National Party in, 34, 43, 47, 123; nation-building myth, 67; Pass Laws Act in, 89–90, 172n11; politics in, 52–55, 119–21; race in, 18–21; Racial Classification Board in, 174n19; RNCS in, 23; settler colonialism in, 19; social science in, 157n2; South African Option, 7–8; students in, 70–71; teachers in, 125; transition period in, 6–10; TRC and, 8–10, 29, 55–56, 64; *ubuntu* in, 7, 48, 148–49, 158n13, 169n3; U.S. and, 12; women in, 72, 80, 172n7. *See also specific topics*
South African Communist Party, 159n14
Soweto Uprising, 166n15
structural inequality, 133
structural racism, 8, 61, 68, 111, 128
structural violence, 8

INDEX

students: anger, 66, 133; apartheid and, 39–40, 51–52, *52*, 86–87, 107–11, *108*; behavioral issues with, 96; black Africans as, 19–20, 36–37, 44–46, 111, 115, 144–45, *145*, 154–55; boredom of, 168n22; as "born frees," 107; characteristics of, *150*, 150–51; classroom dynamics, 176n6; consequences and, 133–34; discrimination to, 121–22; at Glenville High School, 58–59, 93, 119; guilt, 6, 19, 59, 61; hierarchies of interest for, 30; history education for, 59–63; identity of, 119–20, 181n18; Indians as, 87–88, 104, 144–45, *145*; inequality to, 105–6; interviews with, 22–23; juxtapositions for, 38–42; knowledge focus for, *27–28*; micro-interactional problems with, 66–67; race to, 79–80, *117*, 117–18; racialized emotions of, 167n21; racism to, 98–99; at Roxbridge High School, 22–24, 40–41, 118; simulations for, 87–93; structural inequality and, 133; teachers and, 17, 47, 64–67, 126–29, 170n14; TRC to, 66–67; whites as, 60–62, 64–65, 110, 144–45, *145*, 162n35, 169n5; white guilt of, 62–63; in Zulu classes, 94–96

Swidler, Ann, 66–67
symbolic boundaries, 163n42
symbolic racism, 115–16

teachers: of apartheid, 34–35, 105; authority and, 17–18; black Africans and, 6; characteristics of, *145*, 145–46; classroom dynamics and, 120–21, 133–34; conflict and, 65–66; equivalences and, 59–63; gender of, 101–2; at Glenville High School, 22–25, 36, 44–48, 153–54; in history education, 38–42; views on Holocaust education, 24–25; interviews with, 149–50; motivations of, 67–68; objectives of, 172n10; observations of, 181n15; race and, 100–101, 168n1, 171n2; resistance to, 81–82; role-playing by, 102–3; at Roxbridge High School, 39–40, 48–50; self-assessment of, 98–100; simulations for, 85–87; strategies used by, 19–20; students and, 17, 47, 64–67, 126–29, 170n14; teacher workshops, 148–49; whites as, 11–12

Third Force, 7

Truth and Reconciliation Commission (TRC): apartheid and, 19–20, 55–56; black Africans and, 9; education and, *28*; EFF and, 97; at Glenville High School, 56–57; higher education and, 147–48; in history education, 10, 64, 149; inequality in, 9–10; interracial trust and, 160n25; Mandela and, 10; narratives from, 66–67; reconciliation with, 8; scholarship on, 8–9; to students, 66–67; Tutu and, 49; *ubuntu* in, 49, 169n3; violence in, 50–51, 57–58, 160n21

Tutu, Desmond, 49

■ 205 ■

INDEX

ubuntu, 7, 48, 148–49, 158n13, 169n3
Umkhonto we Sizwe (MK), 53
United States (U.S.): black history in, 13; civil liberties in, 115–16; civil rights movement in, 5, *27–28*, 29; color-blindness in, 134, 170n12; race in, 20; role-playing violence in, 20, 164n48, 173n16; South Africa and, 12
University of Cape Town, 131–32
University of the Witwatersrand, 132
upward mobility, 132
U.S. *See* United States

violence: assassinations, 159n14, 173n16; in history education, 56–57; interethnic, 7, 159n15; by resistance organizations, 8–9; Sharpeville Massacre, 166n15; in TRC, 50–51, 57–58, 160n21; by whites, 54–55, 59

wealth taxes, 110
whites: as allies, 83–84, 126–27; 169n6; black Africans and, 2–3, 14–15, 39, 51–52, *52*, 82–83, 176n6; equivalences to, 47–52, *52*; at Glenville High School, 71–72, 115–17; interpersonal racism and, 113–14, *114*; at Roxbridge High School, 62–63; in simulations, 71–74; as students, 60–62, 64–65, 110, 144–45, *145*, 162n35, 169n5; as teachers, 11–12; violence by, 54–55, 59
white guilt, 6, 19, 59, 62–63, 66–67, 133
white privilege, 12, 14, 32, 75, 83–84, 111, 134; avoidance of, 49, 68, 79; legacy of, 16
white supremacy, 4, 7, 34, 83, 132, 169n4
white resisters/resistance, 47–52, *52*, 84
white victims, 47–52
why questions, in history education, 38–42
Wilson, Richard A., 9–10
Women's March, 80, 90, 92, 166n15
World War II, 24, *27–28*, 29, 31–32, 151. *See also* Holocaust

xenophobia, 40

Youth Day, 166n17

Zerubavel, Eviatar, 33–34
Zimbabwe, 40
Zulu classes: Afrikaans classes and, 70–71, 74–75, 79, 146; black Africans and, 122; classroom dynamics in, 94–96, 111. *See also* simulations
Zuma, Jacob, 119, 171n3, 175n6

GPSR Authorized Representative: Easy Access System Europe, Mustamäe tee 50, 10621 Tallinn, Estonia, gpsr.requests@easproject.com

www.ingramcontent.com/pod-product-compliance
Lightning Source LLC
Chambersburg PA
CBHW022055290426
44109CB00014B/1106